Preparing for the Rapture
The Next Event on
God's Prophetic Clock

THE
GREAT
ESCAPE

Dr. Jack Van Impe

D0063019

The Great Escape
Copyright © 1998 by Jack Van Impe Ministries

All rights reserved. No portion of this book may be reproduced, stored in a
retrieval system, or transmitted in any form or by any means–electronic,
mechanical, photocopy, recording, or any other–except for brief quotations in
printed reviews, without the prior permission of the publisher.

Scripture quotations used in this book are from the
King James Version of the Bible.

Library of Congress Cataloging-in-Publication Data

Van Impe, Jack.
    The great escape : preparing for the rapture, the next event on God's prophetic
clock / Jack Van Impe
        p.   cm.
    Includes bibliographical references.
    ISBN 0-8499-4073-7
    1.   Rapture (Christian eschatology)   I. Title
BT887.V34 1999   98-41562
236'.9–dc21   CIP

Printed in the United States of America.

Jack Van Impe Ministries   In Canada:
P.O. Box 7004   P.O. Box 1717, Postal Station A
Troy, Michigan 48007-7004   Windsor, Ontario N9A 6Y1

www.jvim.com

ISBN# 0-8499-4073-7

Contents

*35 Most Frquently Asked Questions
about the Rapture*

Contents

Contents

Foreword

During my more than fifty years of ministry conducting crusades in eleven hundred cities in fifty nations as well as producing fifteen hundred programs for radio and television, Rexella and I have received and answered thousands of questions concerning the great prophecies of God's inerrant Word.

As I write this book on the most exciting event in history—the Rapture—I have decided to approach my presentation in a question-and-answer-type format dealing with the most universally asked inquiries covering five decades of ministry.

It is my heart's desire that your eyes be enlightened and your heart stirred with the hundreds of biblical insights that speak of that glorious day when Christ appears in the heavens to take His church home to be with Him. God bless you as the Holy Spirit leads you into an even greater understanding of what our heavenly Father has for you in the pages that follow—and for all eternity.

Maranatha!

Jack Van Impe

Read This First

The next event on God's prophetic clock is the Rapture, a word that is derived from the Latin *rapturo,* meaning, "a snatching away." The Rapture is that dramatic moment when the Lord Jesus Christ comes in clouds of glory to remove from this world all who have died in Christ along with the living from the Day of Pentecost until Christ comes to "snatch" his children upward and home in the twinkling of an eye. First Thessalonians 4:16-18 teaches, "For the Lord himself shall descend from heaven with a shout, with the voice of the archangel, and with the trump of God: and the dead in Christ shall rise first: Then we which are alive and remain shall be caught up together with them in the clouds, to meet the Lord in the air: and so shall we ever be with the Lord. Wherefore comfort one another with these words."

This event will occur at breakneck speed—in the "twinkling of an eye." Scientists at General Electric Company have measured the twinkling in a human being's eye, *and it amounts to eleven-one hundredths of a second.* Those left on earth will not know what hit them. A business colleague will suddenly be gone. A schoolteacher will no longer stand before his or her desk as the chalk falls to the floor. A doctor will not show up for his rounds. There will be no nurses at many hospitals to administer medicine, take pulses, or follow doctors' orders. Dirty dishes will be left in the sink as a housewife disappears from the view of her stunned family. The Rapture will precipitate the greatest traffic jams in history as cars suddenly become driverless and pedestrians run for cover. It will be that moment in history when, without warning, the Lord says, "Come up hither" (Revelation 4:1). *It will be the greatest escape in the history of the world.* There are critics such as Dave McPherson, author of the unbelievable *Pretribulation Origin,* and John Bray who teach that the pretribulational viewpoint only began in 1830 and was propagated by Edward Irving, J. N. Darby, and Margaret McDonald, a retarded girl. He and others have offered $1,000 to any and all who produce one documented statement concerning a pretribulation Rapture before the nineteenth century. Should any reader see such a challenge in the future, present your claims as listed below.

St. Victorinus, the bishop of Pettau, wrote a commentary on the Book of Revelation in A.D. 270. He said he saw another great and wonderful sign. "Seven angels having the last seven plagues, for in them is completed the indignation of God. And these shall be in the last time when the church shall have gone out of the midst." St. Victorinus was talking about the Rapture.

Here is more powerful documentation on a pretrib Rapture. The early Christian writer and poet Ephraem the Syrian (who lived from A.D. 306 to 373) was a major theologian of the early Byzantine Eastern Church. To this day, his hymns and homilies are used in the liturgy of the Greek Orthodox and Middle Eastern Nestorian Churches. He also wrote a large number of commentaries that have never been translated into English. Concerning a pretrib Rapture he stated: "All the saints and Elect of God are gathered, prior to the tribulation that is to come, and are taken to the Lord lest they see the confusion that is to overwhelm the world because of our sins." [1]

Thus, this teaching is not a present-day innovation but a doctrinal statement dating back seventeen centuries to St. Victorinus, and twenty centuries back to Jesus and Paul. However, there is more. In the sixteenth century there were also those who expressed absolute assurance of the Rapture. Hugh Latimer, burned at the stake for his faith in 1555, said, "It may come in my days, old as I am, or in my children's days, the saints shall be taken up to meet Christ in the air and so shall come down with him again." Joseph Mede, the great sixteenth-century literalist, understood 1 Thessalonians 4:13-18 to teach the catching up of the saints and even used the word *Rapture.* This also was 250 years before Irving. Darby, and McDonald. While the Rapture is not taught in Matthew, Mark, and Luke, you will find it mentioned twice in the Gospel of John. This is important to remember: Any other time you read about Christ's return in the Gospels, it is not referring to the Rapture. Instead, these are references to the second phase of Christ's return, when He physically comes back to earth to rule over the earth after a seven-year Tribulation period. Where are the two Rapture texts found in the Gospel of John? John 14:1-3: "Let not your heart be troubled: ye believe in God, believe also in me. In my Father's house are many mansions: if it were not so, I would have told you. I go to prepare a place for you. And if I go and prepare a place for you, I will come again, and receive you unto myself; that where I am, there ye may be also." This is not His coming to the earth, but a time when Jesus receives us unto Himself at the great

Rapture—the snatching away—to be with Him in heaven as the seven years of torment play out their unbridled fury on earth.

The second reference to the Rapture is in John 11:25-26. I must confess that I quoted this passage for years and did not really understand it. Christ said: "I am the resurrection, and the life: he that believeth in me, though he were dead, yet shall he live: And whosoever liveth and believeth in me shall never die. Believest thou this?" Jesus is contrasting those who experience death and live again ("the dead in Christ shall rise first," 1 Thessalonians 4:16) with those who never experience death (because "we which are alive and remain" are caught up without dying, 1 Thessalonians 4:17).

In the following pages, we will direct our attention to those events that are leading up to the Rapture, the Rapture itself, and what happens once God's chosen are caught away to be with the Lord. The Rapture is not science fiction. It's a coming reality. The good news for the person who is prepared is—when the Rapture comes, believers will go home to be with the Lord and evade earth's horrendous seven years of Tribulation. The believer in the Lord Jesus Christ will, at long last, be the recipient of that blessed hope. There will be no more tears, no more suffering, and no more dying for those who have received their new, glorified bodies— bodies without sin or sickness for all eternity. It is from this perspective—the pretribulation point of view—that I approach this subject with godly reverence. Friends, read these pages and be encouraged that the great and glorious day of Christ's appearing is at hand.

Question 1

What is the correlation between Christ's resurrection and the Rapture of the Church? Why, even at the "time of the end," will the world go on eternally?

Paul's message to the church in Corinth (1 Corinthians 15) is strong and beautifully stated. Twenty centuries later, it is still impossible to overstate the profound importance of our Lord's resurrection to our faith. If Jesus had not risen from the dead as the Bible states, then all who had and have fallen asleep (died in Christ) have perished and our hope for eternal life is gone. If Jesus had remained in the grave, so would we. But praise God; He is risen from the dead. We serve a risen, living Savior. Think for a moment about what happened when Christ rose from the grave. What was left behind? All that was found in that sepulcher were our Lord's grave clothes. What is the significance of that fact? In 1 Corinthians 15:23, it says Christ is the "first-fruits" of the resurrection. In the following text it states, "They that are Christ's at his coming" will follow. The answer is there in black and white. Since Christ's clothes were left behind, ours will be left behind also. Those that belong to Christ at the time of His coming will be bodily translated into heaven just as Jesus was, leaving behind the rags of sin for new robes of righteousness.

The Great Escape

He Will Return as He Left

When Jesus Christ comes to call us home at the time of the Rapture, He will come to receive us exactly as He left. How did He leave? He left bodily, ascending into the clouds. Acts 1:9-11 says, "And when he [Jesus] had spoken these things, while they beheld, he was taken up; and a cloud received him out of their sight. And while they looked stedfastly toward heaven as he went up, behold, two men stood by them in white apparel; Which also said, Ye men of Galilee, why stand ye gazing up into heaven? This same Jesus, which is taken up from you into heaven, shall so come in like manner as ye have seen him go." In other words, if we can prove that Jesus ascended into heaven bodily, then we need go no further to prove that He is coming back bodily. Why? Because the Bible says *He is coming back exactly as He left*. After spending three days in the grave. He rose and stood on the earth in His new body. In Luke 24:39, He says to some of His followers, "Behold my hands and my feet, that it is I myself: handle me, and see; for a spirit hath not flesh and bones, as ye see me have." In verses 41-43, He says, "Have ye here any meat? And they gave him a piece of a broiled fish, and of an honeycomb. And he took it, and did eat before them." This is Christ in His new resurrected body, a body that could be seen, a body that could be touched, and a physical being that could eat food. It is a picture of what all believers will have at the time of the Rapture. How quickly will it happen? "Behold, I shew you a mystery," the Bible tells us in 1 Corinthians 15:51-53. "We shall not all sleep, but we shall all be changed. In a moment, in the twinkling of an eye, at the last trump: for the trumpet shall sound, and the dead shall be raised incorruptible, and we shall be changed. For this corruptible [the dead] must put on incorruption, and this mortal [the living] must put on immortality." This is going to be a glorious event because we shall be changed to be like Jesus. The psalmist said in chapter 17, verse 15, "I shall be satisfied, when I awake, with thy likeness." In Philippians 3:21, Paul says that God will change our vile bodies—not leave them behind but change them—so that they may be fashioned like unto His glorious body. In 1 John 3:2, it says that when we see Jesus, we shall be like Him, "for we shall see him as he is."

The "Fourth" Rapture

Did you know that Jesus was not the first person to be raptured from this earth? In fact, when the Rapture occurs, it will be the fourth occurrence documented in the Bible. The first was Enoch in Genesis 5:24, "And Enoch walked with God: and he was not; for God took him." In Hebrews 11:5, Paul adds, that "by faith Enoch was translated that he should not see death." He was raptured, caught up in the twinkling of an eye, without dying. The second documented rapture is Elijah in 2 Kings 2:11. Elijah was caught up by a whirlwind into heaven. He, too, never saw death, a foreshadowing of what we believers will experience on the day when our Savior catches us up in the clouds. Then, of course, Jesus was raptured away in Acts 1:9, "And when he had spoken these things, while they beheld, he was taken up; and a cloud received him out of their sight."

When Elijah was caught up, angels and chariots of fire came to get him. I believe that angelic hosts may also come after those of us who ascend in the Rapture. Why? Because every believer, not just Elijah, has his or her own ministering angel (Hebrews 1:14). These heavenly bodies could come to whisk us home in the twinkling of an eye. Luke 16:22 provides a precedent for us, "And it came to pass, that the beggar died, and was carried by the angels into Abraham's bosom." Let me ask you this: Is all this something that should frighten us? Excite us, yes. Frighten us, no. As I field scores of Rapture questions each month on television and radio, I discover unfortunately, that many people today are facing the approach of Christ's return with unnecessary fear and foreboding. There is an anticipation, largely promulgated by the secular media, that we may be nearing the end of the world. There is anxiety and hopelessness everywhere. The world seems to get just a bit uglier every day as crime increases, wars break out, and immorality rules the day. Yes, those are the facts. Things *will* get much worse before they start to get better—during the Millennium. But the believer need not despair, especially when we remember what Jesus did for us on the cross of Calvary, and how He defeated the last enemy, death (1 Corinthians 15:26). What could be more exciting and encouraging than the idea that some of us will never die? That's why in Titus 2:13, Paul calls the Rapture our "blessed hope." In 1 Thessalonians 4:18, he says, "Comfort one another with these words." Comfort one another, he says, *not frighten one another.*

The World Will Never Disappear

I have been saving the best news for you until last. Here it is: The world is not—I repeat— *is not* coming to an end. The world is not going to disappear in a puff of nuclear smoke in the 21st Century, nor even a thousand years after that. God has shown me something recently to change my thinking 180 degrees concerning this subject. It is now clear to me from Scripture that the world will not even end after Christ's one-thousand-year reign on earth. The world will never end. Isaiah 45:17 is unequivocal when it says that it is a world without end. Paul adds in Ephesians 3:21, "Unto him be glory in the church by Christ Jesus throughout all ages, world without end. Amen." I have discovered 120 texts in recent studies stating that the world will never end—109 in the Old Testament and 12 in the New Testament. Skeptics will no doubt point to Matthew 13:39,49; 24:3; 28:20; and Hebrews 9:26 as proof texts that the world will end. Matthew 24:3 states: "As he sat upon the mount of Olives, the disciples came unto him privately, saying. Tell us, when shall these things be? and what shall be the sign of thy coming, and of the end of the world?" Remember that the New Testament was written in Greek. The Greek translation of that last word is "age," not "world." This age of grace precedes the millennial age; thus, the world is not coming to an end. But this epoch, this age, this era *is* coming to a close. Why? Because it could conceivably be the year that marks the end of the age of grace and the beginning of the millennial age when the King of kings and Lord of lords returns. When he comes, His kingdom holds dominion over the earth for one thousand years. Then He is recommissioned (1 Corinthians 15:24-28) so that His kingdom on earth becomes eternal (Isaiah 9:6-7; Luke 1:32-33; Hebrews 1:8). Since His kingdom is forever and forever upon earth, this old world cannot ever end (Ecclesiastes 1:4; Psalm 104:5).

The Great Escape

The Return of Jesus Is Imminent

We have already noted that long before Christ was born, the Jewish rabbis taught a six-day theory about the future of the world. They believed that the world would face several eras lasting a total of six thousand years, from Adam's creation until the Messiah would come. This theory was based, in part, on Psalm 90:4: "For a thousand years in thy sight are but as yesterday." Since God created the world in six days and rested on the seventh day, they reasoned, the world would go on for six thousand years followed by a one-thousand-year millennial "rest" period presided over by the Lord Himself. Give this argument some thought: From the creation of Adam until the birth of Christ is a period of four thousand years or four days passed. From Christ's time on earth until now represents approximately another two thousand years or two days. This total of six days is just one more reason to believe that the return of our Lord is imminent. Six-day periods, followed by remarkable transitions, have been important throughout all of Scripture. However, because of calendar miscalculations, I believe the actual timetable falls approximately around 2012.

Note what the Gospel writer says in Matthew 17:1-2, "And after six days Jesus taketh Peter, James, and John his brother, and bringeth them up into an high mountain apart, And was transfigured before them: and his face did shine as the sun, and his raiment was white as the light." Jesus was giving them a preview of what it would be like when He returns as King of kings and Lord of lords as described in Revelation 19:16. When they came down from that mountain, Jesus told them not to tell anyone of these things until after His resurrection. Not only did the ancient Jewish rabbis teach this six-day theory, but so did the Church during the first three hundred years of Christendom. The early church leaders based their belief on 2 Peter 3:8, "But, beloved, be not ignorant of this one thing, that one day is with the Lord as a thousand years, and a thousand years as one day."

Consider the following information once again from the "Epistle of Barnabas."

> And God made in six days the works of his hands; and he finished them on the seventh day, and he rested the seventh day, and sanctified it. Consider, my children, what that signifies, he finished them in six days. The meaning of it is this; that in six thousand years the Lord God will bring all things to an end. For with him one day is a thousand years; as himself testified! saying, Behold this day shall be as a thousand years. Therefore, children, in six thousand years, shall all things be accomplished. And what is that he saith, and he rested on the seventh day, he meaneth this; that when his Son shall come, and abolish the season of the Wicked One, and judge the ungodly; and shall change the sun and the moon and the stars; then he shall gloriously rest in that seventh day. (w. 3-6)

Irenaeus A.D. 140 (Early church father, 1850 years ago)

> "For in so many days as this world was made, in so many thousand years shall it be concluded... and God brought to a conclusion upon the sixth day the works he made...."

The Great Escape

The chronological tables could be off by a number of years. However, we know that the time of the end is near, even at the doors, though we know not the day and hour. Just minutes remain before midnight. The closing day is upon us. Work is about to cease, and we believers are about to rule and reign with the Lord Jesus Christ.

God Will Always Spare His Own

The other great, good news is that God always spares His own from judgment. When the horrendous worldwide flood destroyed everything in sight in Noah's day, Noah told those who were prepared to *come into* the ark (Genesis 7:7). When the judgment fell on Sodom and Gomorrah in Genesis 19:12, the angels told Lot and his family to *come out* of the city. Notice this interesting trilogy: In Noah's day, it was *come in.* In Lot's day it was *come out.* In our day, it will be *come up.* Revelation 4:1. However, as always, only a select group will be rescued from this more heinous period in human history. During the Tribulation Hour that follows the Rapture, all hell will break loose on planet earth. It will be a treacherous time for those who are left behind, primarily because the hindering power of the Holy Spirit within believers will be removed—not the Holy Spirit per se but rather the believers He indwells. Since the Holy Spirit is God and omnipresent (everywhere at all times), He can never be removed (see Psalm 139:1-12). In this light, God's people should be living holy lives. But what about those who are left behind? There are almost no instructions about how to prepare for this post-Rapture period. That is why our ministry has produced Bible-based videos such as *Left Behind? What's Next?* to help those who need to have the facts of life explained to them covering the Tribulation period. More than anything else, this and other videos will hopefully serve as survival helps for those who fail to come to Christ before He returns for His church and bride.

It Will Be Worse Before It Gets Better

How bad will things get during that time of judgment? We have addressed this issue periodically throughout this book. In Revelation 9:18, it says that a third of humankind will be killed by fire, smoke, and brimstone. That, my friends, is nothing less than a first-century way of explaining all-out thermonuclear warfare. Imagine. There are nearly six billion people on the earth today. If one-third of the inhabitants are killed, that is a holocaust representing two billion lives. However, that is only the beginning. In Revelation 6:8, the rider on the fourth horse brings with him a worldwide plague of disease that causes another fourth of humanity to perish. That is another billion of the four billion still alive. Thus half of the human race will be annihilated in this relatively brief period. This portrays the judgment predicted by Jesus in Matthew 24:41 and 42 when He stated, "Two women shall be grinding at the mill; the one shall be taken, and the other left. Watch therefore: for ye know not what hour your Lord doth come." As terrible as that fate sounds, *there is still hope for those left behind.* As long as one is alive there is hope. In the midst of the worldwide carnage and the massive destruction of human life and property, Joel 2:32 and Acts 2:21 remind us, "Whosoever shall call on the name of the Lord shall be saved." There is always hope in Jesus.

For then shall be great tribulation.

Matthew 24:21

Question 2

Pre-, mid-, or postribulational view.
Which position is correct?

T he Bible is truth, it provides peace to troubled souls living in a chaotic world. Because it is a two-edged sword, it cuts through the insignificant and points to what is authentic. Because it is sheer, raw power, it has the dynamic to move the tallest mountains of unbelief. It is a compendium of truth by which we must live and is nothing short of majestic. Yet, there are many interpretations of holy writ. Great controversy continues to surround the subject of the return of Christ for His church—as far as a timetable is concerned. There are essentially three points of view.

Pretribulation View

The pretribulation position, on which this book is based, reflects the following:

The promise to the church in Philadelphia (Revelation 3:10). The Book of Revelation is written chronologically. It sets forth the believer's deliverance from wrath in a beautiful way. Revelation 1:19 states, "Write the things which thou hast seen, and the things which are, and the things which shall be." Presently, the twentieth century finds us in Revelation, chapter 3. John sees the great escape or evacuation of believers in chapter 4, verse 1. He says, "I looked, and, behold, a door was opened in heaven: and the first voice which I heard was as it were of a trumpet talking with me; which said, Come up hither, and I will shew thee things which must be hereafter." I believe this to be the Rapture because the twenty-four elders, picturing the saints of all ages—Old and New Testament believers—are already crowned and casting their rewards at Christ's feet in verses 10 and 11, and believers cannot be crowned until the resurrection of the just occurs (Luke 14:14). Thus, the Rapture has already taken place, the rewards have been distributed, and all is well as the chapter ends.

Then the Tribulation Hour, depicted in Revelation 6, will continue until the Battle of Armageddon, when Christ returns as King of kings and Lord of lords (see Revelation 19:11-16). The crowning of the saints in chapter 4, plus the fact that the Church is conspicuously absent and not even mentioned after chapter 4, is certainly meaningful.

The seven churches of Revelation 2 and 3 represent the professing Church in seven successive eras from the Day of Pentecost to the time of the Lord's return. Each church fits chronologically into its respective place in history. The sixth church, Philadelphia, escapes the Tribulation Hour, but the seventh, Laodicea, is rejected by Christ. True believers, possessing Christ, are kept from the hour of temptation that immerses our entire planet: "I also will keep thee from [not through] the hour of temptation" (Revelation 3:10). Also, "God hath not appointed us to wrath" (1 Thessalonians 5:9).

The case of the twenty-four elders (Revelation 4:1).

Now let's consider another great pretribulational truth—the twenty-four elders. After the "Come up hither" of Revelation 4:1, twenty-four elders are casting crowns at Christ's feet in verses 10 and 11. Then a throne is set up. Around God's throne are twenty-four thrones on which sit twenty-four elders, "clothed in white raiment; and they had on their heads crowns of gold" (Revelation 4:4). Who are the twenty-four elders? *This is of extreme importance for pretribulation proponents:* The twenty-four elders are the representatives of God's people in both Testaments— the saints of all ages. The Book of Revelation unites the representative groups often. For instance, in describing the Holy City in Revelation 21:12-14, the names of the twelve tribes of Israel are posted on the gates, while the names of the twelve apostles are inscribed upon the city's foundation. Now twelve plus twelve equals twenty-four.

In chapter 5, verses 8 through 10, these twenty-four elders do something that is spine-tingling: "[They fall] down before the Lamb [Jesus], having every one of them harps, and golden vials full of odours, which are the prayers of saints. And they [sing] a new song, saying, Thou art worthy [Christ] to take the book, and to open the seals thereof: for thou wast slain, and hast redeemed us to God by thy blood out of every kindred, and tongue, and people, and nation; and hast made us unto our God kings and priests: and we shall reign on the earth."

Here we witness the praise session of the ages—Old and New Testament believers, represented by twenty-four elders, praising the Lamb of God for shedding His blood. Someone says, "Old Testament believers were not saved by the blood." No one—but no one—gets to heaven without the shed blood of Jesus! This is why Acts 10:43 declares,

"To [Jesus] give all the [Old Testament] prophets witness, that through his name whosoever believeth in him shall receive remission of sins." Therefore, Old and New Testament believers, pictured by the twenty-four elders, are singing about the blood in Revelation 5:9 before the seal judgments begin in chapter 6 (the beginning of the Tribulation Hour). The Jews of old looked ahead to Calvary's shed blood as they offered their animal sacrifices while the Church looks back to the Cross as the communion or memorial supper is conducted. Either way, "It is the blood that maketh an atonement for the soul" (Leviticus 17:11).

Since the elders are already crowned—and since no one can be crowned until he is either resurrected if dead, or translated if living—it is obvious that the Resurrection has occurred by the time we reach Revelation 4:10. First Thessalonians 4:16 has transpired. We conclude, then, that the scene in Revelation 4 and 5 is the direct result of the Rapture, the great escape before the judgments begin in chapter 6.

The Holy Spirit, the hinderer, is taken out of the way (2 Thessalonians 2:7-8). Another truth concerning the pretribulation Rapture that needs to be considered has to do with the ministry of the Holy Spirit. Jesus, before departing from earth to heaven, said, "Nevertheless I tell you the truth; It is expedient for you that I go away: for if I go not away, the Comforter will not come unto you; but if I depart, I will send him unto you. And when he is come, he will reprove the world of sin, and of righteousness, and of judgment" (John 16:7-8). It is evident that the work of the Holy Spirit is to convict us and restrain us from sin. The Spirit of God does this through those whose bodies He indwells.

I Corinthians 6:19 states, "What? know ye not that your

body is the temple of the Holy Ghost which is in you, which ye have of God, and ye are not your own?" Every child of God is indwelt by His Spirit: "Now if any man have not the Spirit of Christ, he is none of his" (Romans 8:9). Spirit-indwelt believers have a purifying effect upon the world. They are the "salt of the earth" and the "light of the world" (Matthew 5:13-14). Salt prevents spoilage, and light dispels darkness. Think of the corruption and darkness that will prevail when the salt of the earth and light of the world are removed at the Rapture. No wonder Jesus said, "For then shall be great tribulation, such as was not since the beginning of the world to this time" (Matthew 24:21).

Does the Bible teach such an evacuation of believers? Is there really a great escape before the Tribulation begins? Definitely! The second epistle to the Thessalonians proves this fact. In the first century, some posttribulationists were already sowing seeds of dissent. They said that the Church was already undergoing the trials of the Tribulation. They even produced a falsified letter, forging Paul's name, that stated the Church was in the hour of trial. Recent post-tribulational writers have almost gone as far in falsifying facts. They even print names of people who adopted their viewpoint, and the people "quoted" wonder how they arrived at such a conclusion.

Paul settled the mess by stating in 2 Thessalonians 2:1-8: "Now we beseech you, brethren, by the coming of our Lord Jesus Christ, and by our gathering together unto him. That ye be not soon shaken in mind, or be troubled, neither by spirit, nor by word, nor by letter as from us, as that the day of Christ is at hand. Let no man deceive you by any means: for that day shall not come, except there come a falling away first, and that man of sin be revealed, the son of perdition; Who opposeth and exaketh himself above all that is called God, or that is worshipped; so that he as God sitteth in the temple of God, shewing himself that he is God. Remember ye not, that, when I was yet with you, I told you these things? And now ye know what withholdeth that he might be revealed in his time. For the mystery of iniquity doth already work: only he who now letteth ["hinders"] will let ["hinder"], until he be taken out of the way. And then shall that Wicked be revealed, whom the Lord shall consume with the spirit of his mouth, and shall destroy with the brightness of his coming."

Paul, deeply perturbed by the forged letter, stated in effect, "I understand someone produced a letter, supposedly written by me, stating that the Church is presently experiencing the pangs of the Tribulation Hour. Don't believe that lying prattle. Don't be bothered, bewildered, or shaken over such a distortion of facts. I could not and would not write such a letter, simply because the Tribulation cannot begin until two things occur. First, there must be a falling away, and second, the man of sin must be revealed" (paraphrased).

Scholars of the past rendered the phrase "falling away" as "a catching away." They talked about a time when the law of gravitation would be broken and men would "fall away" via the Rapture to meet the Lord in the clouds. Other scholars believed that the Greek word *apostaias* meant that an apostasized departure from the faith would occur. The important point to consider is that either must happen before the man of sin—the lawless one, the beast of the seventieth week—is revealed. This introduction of the Antichrist to the world will inaugurate the Tribulation Hour. This means that the "day of the Lord" or the Tribulation period cannot begin until this monstrous maniac is identified to earth's citizens. Yet he cannot be revealed until the restraining influence of the Holy Spirit is removed: "He who now letteth ["hinders"] will let, until he be taken out of the way. And then shall that Wicked be revealed (2 Thessalonians 2:7-8).

This does not mean that the Holy Spirit must be removed from the earth. This is impossible because He, as God, is omni-present, everywhere at all times (see Psalm 139:7-11). So it means that His hindering or restraining power over sin—that keeps the Antichrist from mounting the throne— will be removed. This will happen as the Holy Spirit's temples—believers' bodies (see 1 Corinthians 6:19)—are taken from the earth to heaven. Then the "salt of the earth" and the "light of the world" will be removed. This immediately will produce corruption and darkness on an unprecedented scale, allowing the world dictator to come to power. This will begin the Tribulation Hour. Then the "beast" of the ages will rule during earth's bloodiest hour, proclaiming himself as God, the Christ (2 Thessalonians 2:4). He will rule until Christ returns to earth at the conclusion of the seven years. Then "the Lord shall consume [him] with the spirit of his mouth, and shall destroy [him] with the brightness of his coming" (2 Thessalonians 2:8).

The Tribulation is called "the time of Jacob's trouble" (Jeremiah 30:7). "Alas! for that day is great, so that none is like it: it is even the time of Jacob's trouble." This prophet, in chapters 30 and 31, summarizes Israel's endurance in the Tribulation Hour and depicts it as Jacob's, or Israel's, trouble. (Jacob's name was changed to Israel in 2 Kings 17:34.) In Ezekiel chapters 38 and 39 the northern army or

Russian bear comes out of the north against Israel. Eighteen different passages mark Israel as the victim. Ezekiel says, "And thou shalt come up against my people of Israel" (Ezekiel 38:16).

Daniel described this horrible period of Tribulation: "And there shall be a time of trouble, such as never was since there was a nation even to that same time: and at that time thy people shall be delivered" (12:1). Daniel's seventy weeks, of which the Tribulation period is the closing segment, has to do with Israel: "Seventy weeks are determined upon thy people and upon thy holy city, to finish the transgression, and to make an end of sins, and to make reconciliation for iniquity, and to bring in everlasting righteousness, and to seal up the vision and prophecy, and to anoint the most Holy" (Daniel 9:24).

The sixty-nine weeks totaling 483 years—already past—had to do with Israel. Why would God change His method of operation for the seventieth week—the Tribulation Hour? The simple conclusion is that there will be no change. God will return to His original program for the final week. This is again the reason that Satan, upon being cast to earth during the Tribulation Hour, goes after the woman (Israel) who brought forth the man-child (Christ) in Revelation 12:12-14. The voice out of heaven cries: "Woe to the inhabiters of the earth and of the sea! for the devil is come down unto you, having great wrath, because he knoweth that he hath but a short time. And when the dragon saw that he was cast unto the earth, he persecuted the woman which brought forth the man child [Christ]. And to the woman were given two wings of a great eagle, that she might fly into the wilderness, into her place, where she is nourished for a time, and times, and half a time, from the face of the serpent."

Here we see God's loving protection for His covenant people for a time—one year, and times—two years, and for half a time or one-half year. This totals three and one-half years or forty-two months—exactly one-half of the Tribulation period. Verse 17 farther corroborates the fact that Israel is the persecuted one, not the Church, for "the dragon was wroth with the woman, and went to make war with the remnant of her seed [Israelites]." Only antiliteralists and antidispensationalists confuse the issue. They allegorize, spiritualize, and pulverize the truth into mass confusion. They make Jews of all the redeemed or relegate the title of "Israelites" to Americans, Canadians, and other Anglo-Saxons. Little do they realize that there can be no harmony of the Scriptures when one does not rightly divide the word of truth (see 2 Timothy 2:15).

What is the truth? It is that God has *two* elect groups of individuals on this earth—Israel and the Church. Israel is the wife of Jehovah forever (Jeremiah 3:14; Hosea 2:19). The Church is the bride of Christ (Revelation 19:7). Romans 9 through 11 depict Israel's past (chapter 9), Israel's present (chapter 10), and Israel's future (chapter 11). During the Tribulation Hour, all Israel shall be saved (see Romans 11:26). The 144,000 Jewish evangelists (see Revelation 7:4-8) will proclaim the gospel of the kingdom to all the world (Matthew 24:14), and all Israel will accept Messiah (Christ) as Savior and King. Now these Israelites are the *elect*: "As touching the election, they are beloved for the fathers' sakes" (Romans 11:28). This solves the problem of Matthew 24:22, which states, "And except those days should be shortened, there should no flesh be saved: but for the elect's sake [Israelites] those days shall be shortened."

Posttribulationists vehemently cry: "You see, the elect are present for the judgments of the Tribulation Hour." Not so! The fact is that Jehovah chose or elected Israel to be His wife, and Christ chose or elected His people to be His bride, and it is the Father's elect wife experiencing the judgments mentioned in Revelation chapters 6-18.

Concerning Israel, Deuteronomy 7:6 declares, "For thou art an holy people unto the LORD thy God: the LORD thy God hath chosen thee to be a special people unto himself, above all people that are upon the face of the earth." This promise is perpetual. "For the gifts and calling of God are without repentance [or change of mind]" (Romans 11:29). This is the reason that all Israel is going to be saved (v. 26). God keeps His covenants (v. 27), and Israelites are still the Father's "election" (see v. 28).

To the Christians, Christ says, "Ye have not chosen me, but I have chosen you" (John 15:16). We were chosen "before the foundation of the world" (Ephesians 1:4), and our choosing is eternal. Now there is no difficulty whatsoever when men see both elections, but confusion reigns when the two are intermingled, spiritualized, allegorized, and symbolized. Take God for what He states—literally—and the problems vanish.

Deliverance from wrath (Luke 17:26-32). The reason this hope is blessed or happy is that the Church escapes the turmoil of earth's most devastating hour. This fact is confirmed by the teaching of Jesus. He said that the days of the Son of man would be like the days of Noah and Lot (see Luke 17:26-32). In Noah's day, Enoch, a type of the Church, was evacuated before the judgment of the Flood, while Noah, a type of Israel, was preserved through it. Lot, in his removal to Zoar before the fires fell, is also a type of the escaping Church before atomic incineration begins.

Upon examining the story of Lot in Genesis 18:23-32, we discover that God informed Abraham that He would destroy the cities of Sodom and Gomorrah. Abraham immediately began bargaining with the Lord: "Wilt thou also destroy the righteous with the wicked? Peradventure there be fifty righteous within the city: wilt thou also destroy and not spare the place for the fifty righteous that are therein? That be far from thee to do after this manner, to slay the righteous with the wicked: and that the righteous should be as the wicked, that be far from thee: Shall not the Judge of all the earth do right?" (Genesis 18:23-25).

Abraham finally got the figure down to ten righteous people, but there were not even ten who were undefiled. Therefore, God had to destroy the cities. Lot and his family, however; survived because God had another plan—the great escape. The angels removed Lot and his family from the city and took them to Zoar. Now listen to this surprising statement from God in Genesis 19:22: "I cannot do any thing till [Lot] be come thither." God had to remove His people before He rained judgment upon the world of the ungodly. Then, and only then, did the Lord rain "upon Sodom and upon Gomorrah brimstone and fire from the LORD out of heaven; And he overthrew those cities, and all the plain, and all the inhabitants of the cities, and that which grew upon the ground" (Genesis 19:24-25).

As it was in the days of Lot, so shall it be in the day of the Son of man, or when the Son of man returns. Whether it is the great escape for the Church or the preservation of the Israelites through the Tribulation, God's promises cannot fail.

The day of great wrath (see Revelation 6:17) will be

meted out to sinners who store up, treasure up, or accumulate "wrath against the day of wrath" (Romans 2:5). But this wrath will be only for the wicked. Paul wrote, "[God] delivered us [Christians] from the wrath to come" (1 Thessalonians 1:10), and again: "For God hath not appointed us to wrath, but to obtain salvation by our Lord Jesus Christ" (1 Thessalonians 5:9).

This salvation from wrath cannot be the eternal deliverance from hell because the Christian already has that without Christ's return. The moment a person believes, he is delivered from condemnation and "is passed from death unto life" (John 5:24). Because of it, "There is therefore now no condemnation to them which are in Christ Jesus" (Romans 8:1). The deliverance from wrath in 1 Thessalonians 1:10 has to do with Christ's return because the text states, "[We] wait for his Son from heaven... which delivered us from the wrath to come." It does not take the return of Christ to deliver us from the wrath of hell—salvation instantaneously accomplished this. But the coming of Christ delivers us from the wrath of the coming Tribulation Hour. This is how God will "keep [us] from the hour of temptation, which shall come upon all the world" (Revelation 3:10).

The Church—the body and the bride (Ephesians 5:30). Now let's look at Christ's church—His body and His bride. Will the Church go through the administration of God's wrath upon the earth? I believe not. Millions of believers are already in heaven. All who have died "in Christ" during the past two thousand years are already with Christ. Paul said, "To be absent from the body [is] to be present with the Lord" (2 Corinthians 5:8). Why should a handful of believers experience God's wrath while millions who lived and died during the last two thousand years enjoy the blessings of heaven during the Tribulation? For God to have 99 percent of His church with Him while 1 percent suffer untold agonies would be inconsistent.

Since the Greek word *ecclesia,* translated "church" in English, means "a called out assembly," could not this definition extend to the very hour when the final "called out assembly" meets the other 99 percent of the Church already in glory? Why should a minority suffer God's vengeance while the others watch from heavenly places? We are also members of Christ's body. "We are members of his body, of his flesh, and of his bones" (Ephesians 5:30).

Should 99 percent of His body in heaven rejoice while the remaining 1 percent upon earth suffer? Perish the thought. In fact, since Christ is the head of the Body, He would actually be administering wrath to His own body if He left part of that body on earth for the Tribulation period. Believers are also Christ's bride. Should 1 percent of the believers (constituting the Bride) languish in anguish while 99 percent abide at His side? Let's be consistent in our thinking! Love demands that all the remaining 1 percent join the 99 percent already in His presence, completing the Church, the Body, and the Bride.

This same Church, Body, and Bride must go through a time of examination called the Judgment Seat of Christ. The Bride also experiences the marriage supper of the Lamb before returning with Christ to the earth. The posttribulation adherents teach a "yo-yo theory"—up and down, going to meet Christ and returning instantly—and have no time interval for this judgment-seat examination or the marriage. It takes time to investigate God's people. Second Corinthians 5:10 states, "For we must all appear before the judgment seat of Christ; that every one may receive the things done in his body." This is an impossibility in the posttribulation arrangement of events because millions cannot be investigated in less than one second or "the twinkling of an eye" (1 Corinthians 15:52). The "bob up to meet Him and bob down to reign" theory, if true, wipes out the intervals of time demanded for the judgment seat of Christ and the marriage.

I believe it is logically and abundantly clear that there will be a Rapture and that it *must* come *before* the Tribulation period. Common sense demands it; confusion reigns without it. Soon the Lord will break through the clouds. His church, body, and bride will be united with members already in His presence, for "them also which sleep in Jesus will God bring with him" (1 Thessalonians 4:14). Then all the Church is investigated and prepared "as a chaste virgin to Christ" (2 Corinthians 11:2) to enjoy the marriage supper and honeymoon.

The Most Powerful Argument For A
Pretribulation Rapture

The final and greatest argument for a pretribulation Rapture is based on Matthew 25:31-46. In this text Christ returns to earth and judges the nations. At this point of time there are two groups present—the saved and the lost. The lost are condemned to everlasting punishment (Matthew 25:41, 46), whereas the saved are invited to enter the kingdom for the thousand-year reign with Christ (Matthew 25:34; Revelation 20:4).

Now, supposing the Rapture occurred at this juncture as postmillennialists teach, who would then be left to reign with Christ upon earth? At the Rapture believers receive glorified bodies (1 Corinthians 15:51-54; Philippians 3:21; 1 John 3:2-3). These bodies, as Christ returns to earth, remain in the Holy City, the new Jerusalem, hovering above the earth for the entire one thousand years (Revelation 21:9-22:5). That being the case, no one would be left to rule on earth if all the saved were raptured and translated, receiving their eternal spiritual bodies at the hour Christ returns to earth. In fact, there could be no Millennium if this theory were followed to its ultimate conclusion. I repeat—if posttribbers are correct, the saved are translated into spiritual bodies while the lost are sent into eternal punishment. This leaves no one to rule and reign with Christ for the one thousand years. On the other hand, if the Rapture occurs before the Tribulation period begins, the riddle is solved. Here's why. There will be multitudes, yes millions upon millions converted during earth's most horrendous hour because this is the time when God's spirit is poured out upon all flesh (Joel 2:28; Acts 2:17), and the greatest revival in history occurs. Revelation 7:9 states: "A great multitude, which no man could number, of all nations, and kindreds, and people, and tongues, stood before the throne, and before the Lamb, clothed with white robes, and palms in their hands." When asked who these tens of millions are, the answer is: "These are they which came out of great tribulation, and have washed their robes, and made them white in the blood of the Lamb" (v. 14). These are the millions who go into the kingdom in earthly bodies for Christ's millennial reign (Matthew 25:34; Revelation 20:4). This is the only position that makes sense and fits the situation of a coming Millennium composed of believers ruling and reigning with Christ in earthly bodies.

The Great Escape

Midtribulation View

According to this view, Christians would pass through the first half of the Tribulation but be raptured at the seventh trumpet judgment. This position, however, does not hold up since it ignores the biblical teaching of imminence—a view that asserts the return of Christ will occur unannounced, at any given moment. This theory is so unpopular today that little space is needed to cover the subject—just enough to describe the viewpoint.

Posttribulation View

This view does not look for Christ to come for His own until after the Tribulation. According to this theory, the Church should not be looking for the blessed hope of the return of Christ, but rather to the appearance of the Antichrist and the indescribable judgments and horrors of the Tribulation period.

Surely no reasonable, rational thinker will disagree with the facts presented thus far concerning the pretribulation Rapture.

Then we which are alive and remain shall be caught up together with them in the clouds, to meet the Lord in the air: and so shall we ever be with the Lord.

1 Thessalonians 4:17

Question 3

What validity, if any, should be given to the
prewrath Rapture theory?

In a book titled *The Pre-Wrath Rapture of the Church* by Marvin Rosenthal, this earlier reliable proponent of the pretrib position altered his view and suggested that the Rapture will take place twenty-one months after the time designated by the midtribulationists and five and a half years after the pretribulation position. In other words, the Church would be destined to face the terrors of the Tribulation before the period of God's wrath occurs.

The problem with this view is that rather than the Church looking forward to the return of Christ, the focus now shifts to the fearful expectation of the coming of Antichrist. No longer is the Church safe from the Tribulation, *but is now present during the first three-quarters of this most horrible period in history.* When first presented to the public, this end-time, theological bombshell resulted in enormous confusion and dismay in many theological quarters. While to date it has been largely dismissed as improbable and unbiblical, it is still important to recognize that this position is shot through with speculation and misinterpretation of Scripture—primarily because it tampers with key verses that for more than one hundred years have been the theological bedrock to the understanding of the Rapture and what has, for the most part, been a pre-tribulation view.

For the Christian, the pretrib position must remain para-mount because it encourages us to look forward to that "blessed hope" (Titus 2:13)—that any-moment-return of "the great God and our Saviour Jesus Christ." The pretrib view promises that Christians will not endure the great terror of that day when Antichrist rules, when hordes of pestilences invade our world, when incurable diseases strike humankind with abandon, and when the atmosphere of earth as we know it deteriorates to where planet earth is unlivable and the air not fit to breathe.

The prewrath view puts Christians in the heat of battle. The brilliant scholar Dr. Gerald B. Stanton writes: "Rosen-thal contradicts himself on the extent of God's wrath and the time of the Second Coming of Christ. While his sincer-ity may be beyond question, many of his definitions appear to be homemade and supporting evidence is completely inadequate. ... Rosenthal is in serious error when he at-tempts to set the time of the Rapture three-fourths of the way through the seven years of judgment and wrath, some 1,890 days after the Anti-Christ makes his unparalleled covenant with Israel. . . . The Lord's people should not be confused by vehement argumentation designed to set the day of His appearing."[1]

If Rosenthal were correct in his assumptions, a prewrath Rapture would be the Christian's ultimate nightmare, hard-ly the "blessed hope" promised in Scripture. Tim LaHaye makes the point: "It would be a non-event, for there would be few if any Christians left to rapture at this time. Could any Christian take Antichrist's mark and thus survive to be raptured? Indeed not. Revelation 14:9-10 makes it clear that 'those who worship the beast and his image, and receive his mark' will be consigned to hell."[2] Well said.

Since the publication of Rosenthal's book, virtually every reviewer has brought its limitations and biblical inaccuracies to light—primary among them the issue of imminency. The prewrath theory destroys the sense of expectation, demotivates the body of Christ, and puts the believer's focus on evil rather than good. The only solace given to Christians in the prewrath theory is that they will be raptured before the great Battle of Armageddon—small comfort since the Church would have already endured the worst of the great Tribulation judgments. Fortunately, while disruptive in some circles over the years, Rosenthal's theory has never gained ardent followers.

According as he hath chosen us in him before the foundation of the world, that we should be holy and without blame before him in love: Having predestinated us unto the adoption of children by Jesus Christ to himself, according to the good pleasure of his will.

Ephesians 1:4-5

Question 4

Who are the "elect" of Matthew 24:22?

Posttribulationists (those who believe the Church of Jesus Christ will endure the terrible period of the Tribulation) like to use this verse—"Except those days should be shortened, there should no flesh be saved: but for the elect's sake those days shall be shortened" (Matthew 24:22)—saying this passage proves the Church will remain on earth because we are the "elect." Nothing could be further from the truth. Many do not realize that God has two elect groups on earth. There is the Church (see Ephesians 1:4; 1 Peter 1:2), but that is not the group referred to in Matthew 24:22. How do I know this? Isaiah 42:1 speaks of *the Jews* as God's elect. So does Isaiah 45:4; 65:9; and 65:22.

How does one know that the Jews are the elect for whom the days are being shortened in Matthew 24:22? It's important at all times to keep the biblical text in context, and this is especially true here. First of all, this elect group is to flee from Judaea to the mountains. Judaea is the Holy Land, the area where Christ walked and ministered in human flesh (see Matthew 24:16). They are not to flee on the Sabbath day *(shabbat)* (Matthew 24:20). According to Exodus 31:13, the Sabbath day is to be eternally practiced by the Jews. In Mark 13:9, we find that they are beaten in the synagogues... not in the churches. We don't meet in synagogues because we are the Church (see Acts 2:47).

Finally, all these events take place in the area of Jerusalem (see Luke 21:24). The elect, therefore, at this time in history, are Jews, God's chosen people, the Israelites. Because of their history of rejecting Jesus Christ as Messiah (Savior), God, in His foreknowledge, has set up a different schedule for the Jews as a nation.

Because the true Church, all born-again believers, wholeheartedly accept Christ as Savior (John 1:11-12), they are called to heaven to escape the Tribulation period, or Time of Jacob's Trouble. During this time of disillusionment and despair, the Jews as a nation will finally recognize Jesus Christ as Messiah and King in the midst of their suffering (Romans 11:26). This clarifies Matthew 24:22, which states, "But for the elect's sake [Israel, Deuteronomy 7:6-7] those days shall be shortened."

The judgment seat of Christ for the Church then occurs in the heavenlies as the Tribulation judgment hits the earth with massive force. Both *elect* groups are being prepared for the Millennium—one in heaven, the other upon earth. At the conclusion of this Time of Jacob's Trouble, Christ returns with an army of believers and judges the nations on the basis of their rejection of Christ and their treatment of Israel (Matthew 25:31-46).

And I heard the number of them which were sealed: and there were sealed an hundred and forty and four thousand of all the tribes of the children of Israel.

Revelation 7:4

Question 5

Who are the 144,000?
What is their role in the great revival to come?
When will that revival take place?
Before or after the Rapture?

In one of the best books in print on the last days, *Escape the Coming Night,* by Dr. David Jeremiah, the author titles one of his chapters "Revival during Hell on Earth." What an apt description of the Tribulation. It will indeed be hell on earth—something we have already described, but that we'll continue to refer to throughout this book. Here's how Dr. Jeremiah describes the Tribulation Hour judgment of a "groaning planet."

> First, the white horse gallops onto the world scene carrying the man of deception, the coming world dictator; second, the red horse claws the air, abolishing any semblance of peace on earth; third, the black horse appears, creating hunger and economic disaster; fourth, the pale horse spreads deadly plague in its path. The fifth seal reveals the martyrs of the Tribulation, and the sixth seal unleashes one of the most devastating earthquakes. What a gloomy backdrop! No wonder the question is asked, "Who is able to stand?" [1]

Who indeed? Monstrous catastrophes will afflict the earth and its people. But then, we see that God sends His angels to seal His people off from final judgment. A reprieve, it seems. Light at the end of a dark tunnel. Once again God protects His own—even as He spread His covering wings over Noah and his family, shielding them from extinction; Rahab the harlot, carried to safety by means of a sturdy scarlet rope; Daniel spared from a den of hungry lions; Moses swept to safety from the bulrushes of Egypt; Lot and his family rescued before the terrible fire fell on Sodom; and the protection of Israel's children through a dabbing of blood on the doorposts of their Egyptian homes. God has provided protection for His people—the children of Israel—throughout the annals of biblical and secular history. Now He promises to protect them once again—during the end times—giving them the opportunity to know the Messiah they so long rejected.

Who will be the minister of God's salvation during this time? The Jews themselves—God's chosen people. Scripture gives ample proof that God can do anything at any time. I do not expect there will be a great revival before the Rapture because 2 Timothy 3:13 states, "Evil men and seducers shall wax worse and worse, deceiving, and being deceived." John also spoke about the latter-day Church in Revelation 3:15-16: "I know thy works, that thou art neither cold nor hot: I would thou wert cold or hot. So then because thou art lukewarm, and neither cold nor hot, I will spue thee out of my mouth."

Presently some of our churches are so cold that we could have signs above the doors stating: First Church of the Deep Freeze, Dr. Jack Frost, Pastor. However, there is going to be a great revival. It will occur during the seven-year Tribulation period when 144,000 Jews (Revelation 7:4-8) will circle the globe, preaching the gospel of the kingdom (Matthew 24:14), declaring the good news: The King is coming! At that time, the Bible says, "All Israel shall be saved" (Romans 11:26). That means Jews. But when one gets to Revelation 7:9, it is a "great multitude." Who are they? These are the ones who emerged from the Great Tribulation "and have washed their robes, and made them white in the blood of the Lamb" (v. 14). They have trusted in the blood of the Lamb. They have been cleansed. Both Jews and Gentiles are saved during the greatest revival in history, because at that time, God says, "I will pour out my spirit upon all flesh" (Joel 2:28). Yes, there will be a great revival, and it will occur after the Rapture. In all probability, the Rapture will convince many that all these things they heard about Jesus and the Bible are, in fact, true, persuading them to want to know the Lord before it is too late.

Behold, I shew you a mystery; We shall not all sleep, but we shall all be changed. In a moment, in the twinkling of an eye, at the last trump: for the trumpet shall sound, and the dead shall be raised incorruptible, and we shall be changed.

1 Corinthians 15:51-52

Question 6

Could there be a "partial" Rapture?

The simple answer is no. Some teach that only the perfect will be evacuated during the Rapture, but this is contrary to the teaching of God's Word. Many base this teaching on Hebrews 9:28—"Unto them that look for him shall he appear the second time without sin unto salvation"—saying that the Rapture is only for those who are watching. Such a premise is at odds with the rest of the Bible. We must always keep the study of the Rapture in biblical context. It's been wisely said that one cannot take a text out of context without creating a pretext. Every verse on the subject must be considered before a valid conclusion can be reached regarding a doctrine.

First John 2:28 tells the other side of the story: "And now, little children, abide in him; that, when he shall appear, we may have confidence, and not be ashamed before him at his coming." This verse begins with the terminology of His appearing and ends with the statement of His coming. It says that when He comes to snatch us into His presence in the twinkling of an eye, there will be many who are ashamed. The conclusion is if they were perfect, they would not be ashamed. So the idea that one must lead a sinless life to be accepted as part of the Body or Bride for the Rapture does not agree with the rest of the Bible.

So let me repeat this important statement. One is not ashamed if he is perfect. Therefore, the imperfect are raptured. The Bible also reveals that there are persons who are saved by fire standing before the Lord (see 1 Corinthians 3:15). They made heaven "by the skin of their teeth," so to speak. The only way any of us can stand in a perfected state before Jesus Christ in that hour is through the merits of His shed blood. Second Corinthians 5:21 declares, "For [God] hath made him to be sin for us, who knew no sin; that we might be made the righteousness of God in him." This is our only perfection. In addition, the Bible states that every believer is a member of the body of Christ. Should only those who meet a certain standard of spirituality be taken, the body of Jesus Christ would be dismembered and disfigured. This is impossible. First Corinthians 15:51-52 states that "we shall ALL be changed, in a moment, in the twinkling of an eye, at the last trump" (emphasis added).

The partial Rapture view, by definition, denies the teaching on the unity of Christ's body. First Corinthians 12:12-13 says, "For as the body is one, and hath many members, and all the members of that one body, being many, are one body: so also is Christ. For by one Spirit are we all baptized into one body, whether we be Jews or Gentiles, whether we be bond or free; and have been all made to drink into one Spirit." What is the message of this verse? All believers are united together to form the entire body of Christ, who is the head. Perhaps most disturbing, however, is that the partial rapturist must place a segment of the body of Christ *in* the Tribulation period. We've already indicated in several places that this cannot happen. The Body of Christ will have no limbs or organs missing on the glorious day the Rapture occurs.

*So likewise ye, when ye shall see all these things,
know that it is near, even at the doors.
Verily I say unto you. This generation shall not pass,
till all these things be fulfilled.*

Matthew 24:33-34

Question 7

What relationship exists between the Rapture, the Revelation, and prophetic signs?

What relationship exists between the Rapture, the Revelation, and prophetic signs? Where do they fit into the schedule of events described in God's Word? Many believers think the *signs* point to phase one, the Rapture, because they identify the snatching away as the Second Coming of Christ. As we noted earlier, doctrinally speaking, this cannot be so. The actual Second Coming of Christ is the second phase, the Revelation, or the revealing of Christ to the inhabitants of earth. Since He came to earth at His first advent, He must come to earth at His second advent. The Rapture is not Christ's appearance upon earth, but a meeting in the heavens—an intermediary evacuation of believers from earth before the storm. Seven years later, Christ comes to earth, touching down on the "mount of Olives" (Zechariah 14:4).

The prophetic signs, then, point to Christ's return to earth with His saints at the close of the Tribulation Hour— not to the Rapture. Here is how you can be assured this interpretation is accurate. Take two Bibles and place them side by side. Open one to Revelation 6, where the signs begin to be fulfilled. Then open the other to Matthew 24, Mark 13, and Luke 17 or 21, where Christ's prophetic predictions are recorded. The inescapable conclusion is that the signs are identical. The Church is taken in Revelation 4, and the signs take place two chapters later. The signs of Revelation 6 are identical to the predictions of Christ in the four Gospels, proving that the signs Jesus gave point to His revelation, the second phase of the Second Coming. Even if there were not a sign yet in existence, we believers could be called home any moment. This is true because each of the signs could occur during the seven-year period following the believers' departure. Remember, the signs point to Christ's Second Coming to earth (Revelation 19).

I believe we may go to be with our Lord at any moment because Jesus said, "When ye shall see all these things [signs—not one, not two, but all the signs occurring simultaneously], know that it is near, even at the doors" (Matthew 24:33). What is near when a person sees all the signs occurring? Christ's return to earth, the Revelation, phase two. When this happens, all believers will return with Him. All the signs pointing to the return of Christ with His saints— the return of the King with His armies—are already in their beginning stages. Thus, the signs say that we, too, are coming back with the Lord soon. How can this be as long as we are still present on earth? There is but one logical conclusion. We must be removed *soon* through phase one, the Rapture, to return with Christ, via phase two, the Revelation.

After this I looked, and, behold, a door was opened inheaven: and the first voice which I heard was as it were of a trumpet talking with me; which said, Come up hither, and I will shew thee things which must be hereafter.

Revelation 4:1

And I saw heaven opened, and behold a white horse; and he that sat upon him was called Faithful and True, and in righteousness he doth judge and make war.

Revelation 19:11

Question 8

What differences are there between the Rapture and the Revelation?

The Rapture

We referred to this earlier, but because it remains one of the most misunderstood areas of end-time teaching, I want to deal with it in depth, buttressed by key passages of scripture, to give you a clear distinction between the two events. Many believers are unaware that there are *two stages or phases* within the process of the Second Coming—the Rapture and the Revelation—and that these events are separated by a seven-year period. I believe the Rapture is the next occurrence on God's calendar. This Rapture is the literal, visible, and bodily return of Christ in the heavens. Acts 1:9-11 states: "And when he [Jesus] had spoken these things, while they beheld, he was taken up; and a cloud received him out of their sight. And while they looked stedfastly toward heaven as he went up, behold, two men stood by them in white apparel; which also said, Ye men of Galilee, why stand ye gazing up into heaven? this same Jesus, which is taken up from you into heaven, shall so come in like manner as ye have seen him go into heaven."

Has Christ already returned? Some cultists declare that He came in 1914 or 1918 as an invisible spirit. This is nonsense! The Bible declares that Jesus shall return as He left. A person can easily know how He left by studying Luke 24:39. Christ, in His new, resurrected body, said, "Behold my hands and my feet, that it is I myself: handle me, and see; for a spirit hath not flesh and bones, as ye see me have." He adds in verse 41, "Have ye here any meat?" The disciples gave Christ a piece of broiled fish and honeycomb, which He took and ate before them (w. 42—43). The risen Savior had a body of flesh and bones—a body that could be seen, touched, and fed. This same Christ, in the same body, shall come in like manner from heaven. When He returns in the heavens, all believers, dead and living, will also be taken bodily to meet Him in the clouds. One day soon, the people of God will disappear from the earth in a blaze of glory.

As a new Christian, I painted a message on the glove compartment of my automobile. It said, "The driver of this car is awaiting the return of Christ. At His coming, Christians will disappear bodily from the earth. Should I suddenly vanish, take over the steering wheel!" I can still remember the look on the faces of hitchhikers as they read my startling message. Some of them declared, "Hey, buddy, the next corner is as far as I go!" It was true then, and it is true today: The unsaved world has great difficulty accepting the glorious teaching of the Rapture. The Christian accepts by faith the declarations of the Word of God concerning this glorious subject. First Thessalonians 4:16-18 states, "For the Lord himself shall descend from heaven with a shout, with the voice of the archangel, and with the trump of God: and the dead in Christ shall rise first: Then we which are alive and remain shall be caught up together with them in the clouds, to meet the Lord in the air: and so shall we ever be with the Lord."

Verse 14 declares that when Christ comes at the time of

the Rapture, He will bring those who sleep (the dead) with Him. At this point, someone may state, "Look here, I've found my first contradiction in the Bible. How can Christ bring the dead with Him (v. 14) and come after the dead (v. 16)?" There are no contradictions in the Word of God. Instead, it is the finite, limited intellect of human beings who are unable to grasp the infinite, unlimited mind of the omniscient God. If one is led by the Holy Spirit and studies under His direction, the so-called contradictions fade into obscurity.

How can Christ bring the dead with Him in verse 14 and come after the dead in verse 16? Here is the solution: When a believer dies, his spirit and soul enter the presence of God, but the body goes into the grave. "To be absent from the body [is] to be present with the Lord" (2 Corinthians 5:8). This soul, absent from the body, is with Christ until the great day when body, soul, and spirit are reunited at the coming of Jesus. So, Christ brings the dead (the soul and spirit) with Him in verse 14 to come after the dead (the body) in verse 16. When "the dead rise first," it is the body—only the body—that comes out of the grave to be reunited with the soul and spirit descending with Christ from heaven.

If the Lord comes to receive the bodies of the dead in Christ, will He leave the bodies of the living in Christ behind? If this were the case, the wisest thing to do at the sound of the trumpet would be to commit suicide. This, however, is not the case. The Bible declares, "The dead in Christ shall rise first: Then we which are alive and remain shall be caught up together with them [the dead] in the clouds, to meet the Lord in the air: and so shall we ever be with the Lord" (vv. 16-17). Thus, we see that the Rapture is a bodily resurrection for the dead and living who are in

Christ, or who are born again.

The entire occurrence is going to take place in half a blink: "Behold, I shew you a mystery; We shall not all sleep [be dead], but we shall all be changed, In a moment, in the twinkling of an eye, at the last trump: for the trumpet shall sound, and the dead shall be raised incorruptible, and we shall be changed. For this corruptible [the dead] must put on incorruption, and this mortal [the living] must put on immortality" (1 Corinthians 15:51-53). In this moment of time, we take upon ourselves immortality and are transformed to be like Jesus. First John 3:2 reports, "[When we see Jesus] we shall be like him; for we shall see him as he is." Philippians 3:21 verifies that our bodies will be changed as we enter into God's presence in whirlwind style. These verses remind us our citizenship is in heaven, where we also look for our Savior, the One who shall change our vile body and fashion it like unto His own glorious body.

There are still those who say, "I don't believe in the Rapture, because the word *rapture* cannot be found in the Bible." Matter of fact, the word *Bible* cannot be found in the Bible either, but this does not disprove the Book's existence. Terms are coined regularly to portray the experiences they picture, and, to review, the word *rapture* comes from the Latin word *rapturo* or *rapio,* which means "a snatching away." The passages above offer proof enough that the Bible teaches a snatching away. Thus, since God tells us there shall be a snatching away, and since *rapturo* translated from Latin to English means "a snatching away," only the willfully ignorant reject such a clear-cut term to describe the first phase of the Second Coming of Christ. Here is an interesting sideline. Jerome, when creating the Catholic Latin Vulgate version, was the first to use the term *rapturo* for the snatching away of 1 Corinthians 15:52.

Hence, the Catholic Church is literally responsible for this glorious term.

The Revelation

The second phase of the Second Coming, described as "the Revelation," will take place seven years after the Rapture. Again, the term *revelation* is a coined word, picturing the truth it depicts. *Revelation* comes from the word *revealing.* When Christ returns to earth, He will reveal Himself to all inhabitants of the globe. Hence, this event is called the Revelation or revealing of Christ. Revelation 4:1 describes phase one of the return of Christ, while Revelation 19:11 depicts phase two. Fix these two chapters firmly in your mind, and prophecy will become a stabilized blessing in your life. The "come up hither" of Revelation 4:1 is the Rapture, the meeting in the air. The appearance of the rider on the white horse and His armies in Revelation 19:11 is the revelation of Jesus Christ. Chapter 4 removes the believer from the judgments described in chapters 6-18, while chapter 19 restores him to his earthly sojourn after the judgments are completed. Chapter 4, depicting the Rapture, occurs before the seven years of tribulation described in chapters 6-18, and chapter 19 describes the return of the King and His people, after the horrendous catastrophes of chapters 6-18 occur. We know this to be true because the Book of Revelation is written chronologically, with the Tribulation Hour taking place in chapters 6-18. Four precedes six, and nineteen follows eighteen. It's that simple. The Church is removed in chapter 4, and the Tribulation follows in chapters 6-18. Then the saints return at the conclusion of the Tribulation Hour in chapter 19.

In addition. Revelation 3:10 states, "Because thou hast

kept the word of my patience, I also will keep thee from [not through (preservation) but from (the Greek—*ek*—OUT of)] the hour of temptation, which shall come upon all the world, to try them that dwell upon the earth." This will be the world's most terrifying hour. All the wars of the past will look like Sunday school picnics in comparison. Jeremiah 30:7 says, "Alas, for that day is great, [there is none] like it." Daniel 12:1: "There shall be a time of trouble, such as never was since there was a nation even to that same time." Joel 2:1-2: "Let all the inhabitants of the land tremble: for the day of the LORD cometh, for it is nigh at hand; a day of darkness and of gloominess, a day of clouds and of thick darkness ... there hath [never] been ... the like." Jesus said in Matthew 24:21, "For then shall be great tribulation, such as was not since the beginning of the world to this time, no, nor ever shall be." When it occurs, fiery incineration will engulf the globe: "The LORD will come with fire" (Isaiah 66:15). "The flaming flame shall not be quenched" (Ezekiel 20:47). "A fire devoureth before them" (Joel 2:3). "The whole land shall be devoured by the fire of his jealousy" (Zephaniah 1:18). "Their flesh shall consume away while they stand upon their feet, and their eyes shall consume away in their holes, and their tongue shall consume away in their mouth" (Zechariah 14:12). "The third part of trees was burnt up, and all green grass was burnt up" (Revelation 8:7). "By these three was the third part of men killed, by the fire, and by the smoke, and by the brimstone" (Revelation 9:18).

The Tribulation Hour lies just ahead for the human race. The saved will be removed before it begins. They are described as taken in Revelation 4:1, and they experience the judgment seat of Christ before the chapter ends. In fact, we find them placing crowns (their rewards) at the feet of

the Savior in verses 10 and 11—two chapters before the
Tribulation period begins. This is proof that the saved are
safe and secure when the judgments begin in chapter 6.
Then, when the blitzkrieg ends in chapter 18, the saved
return with Christ as He appears to the inhabitants of the
earth and becomes their King.

Revelation 19:11-16 gives us a glimpse of the momentous event: "And I saw heaven opened, and behold a white
horse; and he that sat upon him was called Faithful and
True, and in righteousness he doth judge and make war.
His eyes were as a flame of fire, and on his head were many
crowns; and he had a name written, that no man knew,
but he himself. And he was clothed with a vesture dipped
in blood: and his name is called The Word of God. And
the armies which were in heaven followed him upon white
horses, clothed in fine linen, white and clean. And out of
his mouth goeth a sharp sword, that with it he should smite
the nations: and he shall rule them with a rod of iron: and
he treadeth the winepress of the fierceness and wrath of
Almighty God. And he hath on his vesture and on his thigh
a name written, KING OF KINGS, AND LORD OF LORDS."

This is the revealing of Christ to the nations. At His
revelation, every eye will see His glory. "Behold, he cometh
with clouds; and every eye shall see him" (Revelation 1:7).
The armies following Him from heaven to earth are the
saints who were removed from the earth in Revelation 4:1.
They were evacuated before the great holocaust began.
They are the same crowd mentioned in Jude, verse 14: "Behold, the Lord cometh with ten thousands of his saints."
The Hebrews and Greeks had no terminology to describe
millions, billions, trillions, quadrillions, etc. They simply
said, "ten thousands." Thus, the innumerable company of
saints following the Lord to earth are the redeemed.

But, beloved, be not ignorant of this one thing, that one day is with the Lord as a thousand years, and a thousand years as one day. The Lord is not slack concerning his promise, as some men count slackness; but is longsuffering to us-ward, not willing that any should perish, but that all should come to repentance.

1 Peter 3:8-9

Question 9

*My friends do not believe in the "blessed hope"—
the return of Christ to claim His own.
I need additional verses that speak specifically of
the Rapture. Also, what about the "signs pointing
to Christ's millennial reign"?
What does that mean?*

Numerous other New Testament passages speak about Christ's return. For instance, Titus 2:13; "Looking for that blessed hope [the Rapture], and the glorious appearing [the Revelation] of the great God and our Saviour Jesus Christ." Hebrews 10:25 speaks about that great "approaching" day. James mentions the hoarding of gold and silver in the last days: "Ye have heaped treasure [gold and silver] together for the last days" (5:3) and adds in verse 8, "the coming of the Lord draweth nigh." Likewise, Jude declares that, as the Lord returns with His saints, filthy dreamers or false prophets who have denied the Bible will be destroyed (see w. 14-15).

There are also signs in the New Testament that speak of the relationship between Jerusalem and the Gentiles. One group of signs deals specifically with Jerusalem's role in world history as well as the role of the Gentiles. Luke 21:24 declares, "Jerusalem shall be trodden down of the Gentiles, until the times of the Gentiles be fulfilled." In modem English, Christ stated, "Jerusalem will be controlled by Gentile nations and powers until the time of My return." Timothy's grandmother, Lois, in 2 Timothy 1:5 may have mentioned this fantastic prophetical utterance to her grandson, but it did not occur in his lifetime. Generations of Jewish grandmothers probably referred to this sign, but it never occurred in their day. Enter the mockers of Scripture who throw their abusive insults: *Where is the promise of this coming? Since our grandparents' departure, all things continue as they were.* However, remember . . . God "cannot lie" (Titus 1:2). Finally, after nineteen hundred years of waiting—after seventy-five to one hundred generations of grandparents had lived and died, it finally happened. A six-day war was fought from June 5 to 10 in 1967. During the battle, the Jews took Jerusalem—one of the most powerful signs of Christ's return.

What about the six-day theory? Second Peter 3:8-9 contains a tremendous mathematical formula: "Beloved, be not ignorant of this one thing, that one day is with the Lord as a thousand years, and a thousand years as one day. The Lord is not slack concerning his promise, as some men count slackness; but is longsuffering to us-ward, not willing that any should perish, but that all should come to repentance." For years, I have referred to this passage as a mathematical masterpiece. Let us review it together. The promise God keeps is found in 2 Peter 3:4. It is the promise of His coming. Because God "cannot lie" (Titus 1:2), He will come again! His heart of love toward sinners is filled with patience, but soon the day of grace will end. His patience cannot go on eternally. His prearranged timetable must be fulfilled. What is this time frame? Can we mortals know such secrets? Yes, we can! Jesus said, "When ye shall see all these things, know that it is near, even at the doors" (Matthew 24:33). Though we will never know the precise day or hour (Matthew 24:36), we can know God's approximate schedule. How can this be? We read that a thousand years is as a day, and a day is as a thousand years. This is not as mysterious as it sounds. In fact, a few mental calisthenics give us the solution to this often-misunderstood equation.

God created the world in six days (Genesis 1:31) and rested on the seventh day (Genesis 2:2). Since a day is as a thousand years and a thousand years is as a day, we have six days of labor, signifying six thousand years of burdensome toil for humanity, and a final seventh day of rest—the millennial reign of Christ—when they live and reign with Christ a thousand years (Revelation 20:4). The calendar on your wall or in your wallet or purse demonstrates that this timetable is practically fulfilled.

Chronologists such as Archbishop James Ussher have worked strenuously on historical timetables to produce the following information: From Adam's creation to Christ's birth, approximately 4,000 years passed. From Christ's birth to our day, 1,998 years have transpired. This gives us a total of 5,998 years. We are on the threshold of the final day! The six-day theory is not my invention, but rather the theory of scores of church fathers in earlier centuries. With that in mind, I want you to consider the following from the amazing document titled the *Epistle of Barnabas*—missionary with the apostle Paul (see Acts chapters 13-15). He said in A.D. 110—nineteen centuries ago:

> And God made in six days the works of his hands; and he finished them on the seventh day, and he rested the seventh day, and sanctified it. Consider, my children, what that signifies, he finished them

in six days. The meaning of it is this; that in six thousand years the Lord God will bring all things to an end. For with him one day is a thousand years; as himself testifieth saying. Behold this day shall be as a thousand years. Therefore, children, in six thousand years, shall all things be accomplished. And what is that he saith, And he rested the seventh day, he meaneth this; that when his Son shall come, and abolish the season of the Wicked One, and judge the ungodly; and shall change the sun and the moon and the stars; then he shall gloriously rest in that seventh day. (w. 3-6)

Other early Church writings confirm the "signs of a thousand years." Irenaeus, an early church father who lived 1,850 years ago, wrote, "For in so many days as this world was made, in so many thousand years shall it be concluded... and God brought to a conclusion upon the sixth day the works he made." The Jewish Talmud states, "The world is to stand 6,000 years, viz., 2,000 confusion and void, 2,000 with the law, and 2,000 the time of the Messiah." The chronological tables could be off by as much as five to twelve years. However, we know that the time of the end is near, even at the doors, though we are not privy to the day or the hour. One thing is certain: Only a few minutes remain before midnight. Closing time is upon us. The Age of Grace is about to end, and believers are soon to rule and reign with the Lord Jesus Christ.

And now, little children, abide in him; that, when he shall appear, we may have confidence, and not be ashamed before him at his coming. If ye know that he is righteous, ye know that every one that doeth righteousness is born of him.

1 John 2:28-29

Question 10

*Will the Rapture of the Church bring both
Blessing and sorrow?*

Yes. Some will be ashamed (1 John 2:28), and some will be full of joy. That is why, in 1 Thessalonians 2:19, Paul asks, "What is our hope, or joy, or crown of rejoicing?" What is going to bring you and me a great crown? He then answers, "Are not even ye in the presence of our Lord Jesus Christ at his coming?" (v. 19). Paul was saying, "I'm going to present you—those I've won to Christ from Rome to Corinth—before the Lord, and that is going to be my joy." But think of the multitudes who will stand before the Lord empty-handed. These are people who have been saved for years, but have no record of service—none whatsoever. They have never won a single soul to Christ.

There will be no scales at the Great Judgment Day at the end of the world whereby one is admitted to heaven if his good works outweigh the bad and vice versa. A person can be saved only by God's grace (unmerited favor), not through works (Ephesians 2:8-9). Second Timothy 1:9 states: "[God] hath saved us, and called us with an holy calling, not according to our works, but according to his own purpose and grace." However, there *is* a system of balances found in the Scriptures when it comes to rewards. Remember that one is neither saved nor kept by works. He *is,* however, to work because of the salvation he already possesses. Ephesians 2:10 gives clear evidence of this fact: "For we are his workmanship, created in Christ Jesus unto good works." The Christian's works following salvation will be weighed on God's scales and put through His judgmental fire. Thus, a system of addition and subtraction can be found at the judgment seat of Christ. The Bible also plainly states that a Christian can accumulate rewards while he is on earth, and then *lose* them before his death, or before the Rapture, by foolish living. The Bible is clear that a Christian cannot live in sin without suffering the consequences—not the loss of his salvation, but of his rewards.

Remember 1 Corinthians 3:15, "He shall suffer loss: but he himself shall be saved; yet so as by fire." Now consider 2 John 8: "Look to yourselves, that we lose not those things which we have wrought, but that we receive a full reward." Consider also Revelation 3:11: "Hold that fast which thou hast, that no man take thy crown." In 1 Corinthians 9:27, Paul says, "But I keep under my body, and bring it into subjection: lest that by any means, when I have preached to others, I myself should be a castaway." The Greek word for *castaway* means "disapproved" or "put on the shelf." Paul knew he could lose all his rewards for heroic service if he allowed his flesh to rule his life rather than the Holy Spirit. If this could happen to the man who had accumulated more "spiritual points" toward heavenly rewards than any servant of God, it can also happen to you and me.

Second Corinthians 11:23-26 lists Paul's service record: "In labours more abundant, in stripes above measure, in prisons more frequent, in deaths oft. Of the Jews five times received I forty stripes save one. Thrice was I beaten with rods, once was I stoned, thrice I suffered shipwreck, a night and a day I have been in the deep [clinging to life in the ocean]; In journeyings often, in perils of waters, in perils of robbers, in perils by mine own countrymen, in perils by the heathen, in perils in the city, in perils in the wilderness, in perils in the sea, in perils among false brethren."

Paul could have lost all of his rewards had he allowed his flesh to control him instead of the Lord. But he didn't. Hear him again—just before he paid the supreme sacrifice (his life)—in 2 Timothy 4:7-8: "I have fought a good fight, I have finished my course, I have kept the faith: Henceforth there is laid up for me a crown of righteousness, which the Lord, the righteous judge, shall give me at that day [the day of Christ's "bema" or judgment seat investigation]: and not to me only, but unto all them also that love his appearing."

What a contrast to some Christians who find it easier to lie in bed rather than go to God's house; who find it easier not to tithe, not to read the Bible, not to pray, not to win souls, not to live in the Spirit. Their reward will be nothing but ashes. Also to those who have allowed the flesh to take control of their lives, their rewards, earned through years of service, will have been lost because of a foolish unfulfilling habit, a beautiful, flirtatious face, or the desire to travel to heaven via worldly pathways.

I don't know all that will be brought to light at that day, but I do know the first question God will ask is: "Did you bring people into My kingdom?" It is also the last thing Jesus commanded us to do: "Ye shall be witnesses unto me . . . And when he had spoken these things, while they beheld, he was taken up; and a cloud received him out of their sight" (Acts 1:8-9). We will also be asked what we did with our finances. "He which soweth sparingly shall reap also sparingly; and he which soweth bountifully shall reap also bountifully" (2 Corinthians 9:6).

And I John saw the holy city, new Jerusalem, coming down from God out of heaven, prepared as a bride adorned for her husband.

Revelation 21:2

Question 11

Who composes Christ's bride?

T he bride of Christ is made up of every man, woman, and child who has been saved from the Day of Pentecost onward. This includes everyone who has received Christ until the Rapture occurs in 1 Thessalonians 4:16. So from Pentecost to the Rapture, the bride of Christ is formed and evacuated. As we approach that blessed day, I'm often asked, "At what stage in God's prophetic program does the Church, or Bride, presently find herself?" According to Oriental marriage customs, we are now in the *betrothal* stage—promised to Jesus Christ. This is why He wants His people to live holy lives. By doing so, we (the Church or Bride) can be presented as "a chaste virgin" to the Savior (or Bridegroom) as expressed in 2 Corinthians 11:2. I believe we are about to be called into the heavenlies for that great marriage ceremony, because every sign leading to this long-prophesied event is already occurring.

Since every sign for Christ's return to earth is already in progress (we'll later look in some detail at contemporary events that prove this), this great wedding must occur soon. It will not be long before we hear the words, "Come up hither" (Revelation 4:1). Then Revelation 19:7 says, "Let us be glad and rejoice, and give honour to him: for the marriage of the Lamb is come, and his wife hath made herself ready."

Every bride anticipates the joys of a honeymoon. Therefore, the next logical question is, "How long will the honeymoon last for the bride of Christ?" After we are taken up in the Rapture (Revelation 4), we return with Christ in Revelation 19:14: "And the armies which were in heaven followed him upon white horses." Jude verse 14 says, "Behold, the Lord cometh with ten thousands of his saints." Revelation 20:4 says, "And they lived and reigned with Christ a thousand years." The only ones coming back with Him are the Bride—to begin the honeymoon. This does not include, however, the Old Testament saints. John 1:17 says, "For the law was given by Moses, but grace [the new dispensation, or covenant] and truth came by Jesus Christ." Now, concerning the salvation of John the Baptist—he did not become a part of the Bride at Pentecost. He was saved before Pentecost. So Jesus called him a "friend of the bridegroom" (John 3:29). John, then, is considered to be a friend of the Bridegroom but not part of the Bride.

The Church, or Bride, began to be formed on the Day of Pentecost and will be completed at the Rapture. Hence, the Old Testament saints are not members of the Bride or Church. Also, since the Church is evacuated at the Rapture—before the Tribulation begins (Revelation 4:1)—one can clearly see that the Tribulation saints who are martyred during this horrendous period do not constitute part of the Bride or Church. The Bride is definitely that group of blood-washed believers beginning at Pentecost and completed at the Rapture. Both the Old Testament and Tribulation saints are raised when Christ returns to earth, so they may be guests at the marriage supper of the Lamb on earth (see Daniel 12:2; Revelation 4-5).

And he saith unto me, Write, Blessed are they which are called unto the marriage supper of the Lamb. And he saith unto me, These are the true sayings of God.

Revelation 19:9

Question 12

*What is the marriage and marriage supper of
the Lamb and where will they take place?*

The marriage partners at this glorious event include
the Lamb (Christ) (Ephesians 5:25-33) and His bride
(the Church)—both of whom have been in heaven
during the Tribulation Hour. While those on earth have
suffered judgment, the Bride is being investigated in preparation for the wedding (Revelation 19:7). For those who
were unfaithful to Christ during the engagement period
(their years of service upon earth), this will be a moment of
humiliation (1 John 2:28) as every believer will be attired in
the wedding garment he or she made while on earth. The
material will be composed of their good deeds that remain
after the judgment seat has taken place (Revelation 19:7-8).
Righteousnesses rather than *righteousness* is the correct
word in this text. The first term has to do with our works,
the second with the imputed righteousness bestowed upon
believers through Christ (2 Corinthians 5:21).

The marriage itself takes place in heaven toward the
end of the Tribulation period upon earth. The phrase, "the
marriage of the Lamb is come" (Revelation 19:7), signifies
that the Church's union with Christ has been completed

(1 Thessalonians 4:17). From this point on, wherever Christ goes, His beloved bride follows. After the marriage, heaven opens and Christ, mounted upon a white horse, begins His descent to earth for Armageddon followed by His bride, the armies clothed in white linen (Revelation 19:11-14). The place of the wedding reception (marriage supper) is upon earth. After exhaustive study of this great event, I believe that immediately following the marriage in heaven, Christ returns to earth with His bride to begin His millennial reign. Old Testament and Tribulation saints are then raised in order that they may be guests at the marriage supper of the Lamb (Revelation 20:4).

And it shall come to pass in the last days, saith God,
I will pour out of my Spirit upon all flesh: and your sons
and your daughters shall prophesy,
and your young men shall see visions, and your old
men shall dream dreams.

Acts 2:17

Question 13

If an individual has heard the gospel and rejected Jesus Christ—and the Rapture occurs— will that person have another opportunity to accept Jesus as Lord during the Tribulation?

In response to this question, most evangelicals turn to 2 Thessalonians 2:11-12, which states: "And for this cause God shall send them strong delusion, that they should believe a lie: That they all might be damned who believed not the truth." The reasoning among many is that anyone who has ever heard the gospel and rejected it will no longer have a chance to accept the Savior. I no longer believe that. Here's why I do not hold this position. As I was studying Acts 2:17, which repeats the prophetic passage of Joel 2:28, the Holy Spirit revealed something to me. God says, "I will pour out of my Spirit upon all flesh." There will be enlightenment as never before. Then it hit me: This is in the *midst* of the horrific Tribulation Hour, but note what it says in Acts 2:19-21: "And I will shew wonders in heaven above, and signs in the earth beneath; blood, and fire, and vapour of smoke: The sun shall be turned into darkness, and the moon into blood, before that great and notable day of the Lord come: And it shall come to pass, that whosoever shall call on the name of the Lord shall be saved." And this whosoever is identical to John 3:16 where all are invited to salvation. Thus, "whosoever" today is identical to "whosoever" during the Tribulation hour.

However, here's my word of encouragement to you. Do not be distraught or depressed. There is great hope for those whose hearts become softened as we approach the return of our Savior and Lord Jesus Christ. God does not want any man, woman, or child to perish. This is the nature of our heavenly Father (1 Timothy 2:4; 2 Peter 3:9). Nevertheless, things will get alarming as we approach the end of the age. That's why Jesus said in Luke 21:9, "When ye shall hear of wars and commotions, be not terrified: for these things must first come to pass." Who would dare question that these days are already upon us? All the more reason for us to share our faith in Christ with those who heretofore have not believed. An added word of encouragement comes to us when our Lord provides the ultimate word of hope and encouragement in verse 31, "When ye see these things come to pass, know ye that the kingdom of God is nigh at hand." That is the glorious day we all await. Now is the time to share the good news, and in so doing, become part of God's final plan for the ages as He pours out His Spirit on all flesh.

I am he that liveth, and was dead; and, behold,
I am alive for evermore. Amen;
and have the keys of hell and of death.
Write the things which thou hast seen, and the things
which are, and the things which shall be hereafter.

Revelation 1:18-19

Question 14

What prophecies concerning the Rapture are
revealed in the Book of Revelation?

I love this question, because I love the Book of Revelation—one of the most amazing books in the Bible. Penned by John, a man of God, whose hand and heart were guided by the Holy Spirit, end-time events in its pages are presented in precise chronological order. In Revelation 1:19, God states, "Write the things which thou hast seen, and the things which are, and the things which shall be hereafter." Notice the three tenses—past, present, and future. Past—write the things which thou hast seen (chapter 1); present—and the things which are (chapters 2 and 3); future—and the things which shall be hereafter (chapters 4-22). In chapters 2 and 3, John offers a panoramic, historical view of the seven churches. Today we are living in the Laodicean church period described in Revelation 3:15-17. God's statement about this age-ending church is, "I know thy works, that thou art neither cold nor hot: I would thou wert cold or hot. So then because thou art lukewarm, and neither cold nor hot, I will spue thee out of my mouth. Because thou sayest, I am rich, and increased with goods, and have need of nothing; and knowest not that thou art wretched, and miserable, and poor, and blind, and naked." We have already reviewed this verse in an answer to an earlier question.

What a graphic description of Christendom in the 21st Century. Our ranks are filled with lukewarm, indifferent, lackadaisical members. Our services are bogged down with formalism, ceremonialism, and ritualism. On the other hand, some services have become comedy hours and jazz-rock celebrations. Many of our sermons, laced with pleasing platitudes, have little or no effect on the listener. No wonder God wants to regurgitate—spewing the distasteful mass of backslidden parishioners out of His mouth. *All of this precedes Christ's return.* I am convinced this insipid attitude of the Church is a major pre-Rapture sign predicted in the Book of Revelation.

Why do I say this? In Revelation 4:1, we read, "After this [after the pitiful situation of the end-time church is observed] I looked, and, behold, a door was opened in heaven: and the first voice which I heard was as it were of a trumpet talking with me; which said, Come up hither." This is the Rapture, the snatching away, and the call of the Bridegroom for His bride. This must be so because the rewarded believers are already casting their crowns at Christ's feet in verses 10 and 11.

A World on Fire

In the eighth and ninth chapters of the Book of Revelation, we find two unusual predictions concerning the woes of the Tribulation Hour. First, Revelation 8:7 mentions the burning of one-third of the earth. Second, Revelation 9:18 depicts the extinction of one-third of the world's inhabitants by fire, brimstone, and pillars of smoke. Could these prophetic and astronomical figures find fulfillment in our day? The answer is an unequivocal yes. Here is an insight. In statistical surveys in geographical atlases, there are detailed pages of information about continents, land areas, and population figures for every country in the world. In fact, I discovered that Africa, Antarctica, Asia, Australia, Europe, North America, and South America cover a total of 56,889,581 square miles. I decided to divide this figure by three, and the resulting sum was 18,963,194 square miles. This is the amount of land that will burn during the Tribulation period, according to Revelation 9:18. None of this was shocking until I continued my research on the predicted alignment of nations, mentioned in Daniel, chapters 2, 7, and 11, and in Ezekiel, chapters 38 and 39, that would confront each other in the last days. Their combined land area totaled—*one-third of the globe.*

Thus, Revelation 8:7 and 9:18 could become factual events—as current as today's headlines—in the near future. Think of it! This war will lead to Armageddon. It will also occur, according to major Bible scholars, during the Tribulation Hour. The signs of the times are present. How much more proof is needed to convince the lost that Christ's return is very near?

Murder, Drug Addiction, Sex, and Burglary

I wish I could make the list of the impending problems more palatable to your taste, but to do so would not be honest. What is the *cause* for the coming horrible judgment? Why is a God of holiness so angry? Again, the Book of Revelation provides the answers.

The Great Escape

Revelation 9:18-21 predicts the destruction of one-third of earth's billions, and it states the reason why: "Neither repented they of their murders, nor of their sorceries, nor of their fornication, nor of their thefts" (v. 21). This is a portrait of today's society. These sins are already inundating the world. Therefore, if this picture of estrangement from God finds its culmination during the Tribulation era, and presently the identical sins are already flooding the earth, the logical conclusion is that we are swiftly moving toward the time of Tribulation. Again, I remind you, those who believe in Christ as Lord and Savior will not be here to experience the pain of that most terrible moment in history.

The abominations mentioned in verse 21 are self-explanatory, especially the first, third, and fourth sins. They are murder, fornication (prolonged immorality), and stealing. The second, however, needs further explanation. In twenty-seven texts of the Bible, *sorcery* usually means "magic" or "witchcraft." However, there are five occasions in Scripture when it definitely means "drugs": Galatians 5:20 and Revelation 9:21; 18:23; 21:8; and 22:15. In these passages the Greek root word is *pharmakeia.* Translated into English, it means "pharmacy," or simply, "drugstore." The literal meaning of the term is "to become enchanted with drugs." In other words, the world will get its kicks out of drugs during this terrible era. Have I persuaded you yet that the Book of Revelation is as current as today's newspaper? Notice the outline in Revelation 9:21. To be able to afford their unnatural "highs," people will turn to fornication—the selling of their bodies—to pay for their addictions. Thousands more will resort to thievery to support their deadly habits. One further point of interest in this chapter is the tie-in of drugs, fornication, and thievery in connection with demon worship; "They repented not of the works of their hands, that they should not worship devils" (Revelation 9:20). First Timothy 4:1 predicts: "Now the [Holy] Spirit speaketh expressly, that in the latter times some shall depart from the faith, giving heed to seducing spirits, and doctrines of devils." This is happening before our eyes. The world is now in the initial stages of a massive demonic invasion as Satan and his cohorts come from space to earth to wreak havoc (Revelation 12:9). The Rapture is near.

*And the Lord shall scatter you among the nations, and
ye shall be left few in number among the heathen,
whither the Lord shall lead you....
When thou art in tribulation, and all these things are
come upon thee, even in the latter days,
if thou turn to the Lord thy God, and shalt be obedient
unto his voice... he will not forsake thee.*

Deuteronomy 4:27, 30-31

Question 15

What is the Tribulation?
What is the purpose for the twenty-one
Tribulation judgments?

This terrible period of history will be the most horrendous our world has ever seen—seven years of nonstop bombardment. In the midst of this fiery judgment there will be little expression of remorse: Hearts will not be bent toward repentance, with few seeking forgiveness for murder, drug abuse, fornication, sexual promiscuity, or theft (Revelation 9:21). The Tribulation, and the sequential judgments of God, will descend on mankind because of blatant sins committed by humanity. It will be a time of widespread apostasy, coupled with a blatant, wholesale denial of biblical truth, combined with moral chaos, an acceleration of spiritism, persecution, pestilence, and earthquakes. Terrible as all this will be. God has a threefold purpose for this period of human history:

1. To save and allow many Jews who enter the Millennium to experience the fulfillment of the kingdom promises to Israel made by God in the covenants;

2. To save a multitude of Gentiles who will then populate the millennial kingdom;

3. To pour out judgment on unbelieving mankind and nations. The final forty-two months or three-and-one-half-year period is so terrifying that it is called the Great Tribulation (Revelation 7:14).

There is good reason the first half of the Tribulation will be more peaceful. Because Jesus Christ, the Prince of Peace, is soon to return, Satan, the great counterfeiter and ultimate deceiver known as Antichrist, will first present himself as the peace-producing Messiah. Not only will he make himself known to the nations, but he will be universally accepted. Satan will enter the body of a man and proclaim himself as God (2 Thessalonians 2:4). This Antichrist will come into prominence and power by presenting a "peace program" to the nations (Daniel 11:21-24). The contracts will be signed and confirmed (Daniel 9:27).

However, in the middle of the seven-year period, the Antichrist dishonors his treaties and makes the last forty-two months the bloodiest in world history as he honors the god of forces (Daniel 11:38). The Great Tribulation is a time of incomparable judgment (Daniel 12:1; Joel 2:2; Matthew 24:21). A total of twenty-one judgments fall upon the earth. They constitute three series of seven each and are described as the seal, trumpet, and vial (or bowl) judgments (Revelation chapters 6, 8, 9,11,15,16). This is the Time of Jacob's Trouble. Revelation 8:7 and 9:18 clearly reveal a judgment of fire during the Tribulation. This coincides with Psalm 97:3; Isaiah 66:15; Ezekiel 20:47; Zephaniah 1:18; Malachi 4:1, and numerous other passages of Scripture. Both Old and New Testaments agree on the coming of what seems to be a fiery, nuclear holocaust (Revelation 8:7; 9:18). The unequivocal counsel of Scripture promises that the Church will be evacuated before the Tribulation judgment begins.

Alas! for that day is great, so that none is like it:
it is even the time of Jacob's trouble;
but he shall be saved out of it.

Jeremiah 30:7

Question 16

*What Tribulation judgments are specifically
mentioned in the Bible?
How drastic are they?*

The word *judgment* is a fearsome word. It speaks of
finality—such as when the judge of an earthly pro-
ceeding delivers the sentence to the defendant in a
court of law. A judgment is indicative of a period when time
has run out. In a spiritual context, it is when the days and
hours are no longer on the side of the person who denies
God and refuses to accept His Son, Jesus Christ, as Savior.
Taking a hard look at events occurring on today's world
scene, there is no doubt that we are approaching that time
of final judgment. The signs are upon us if we have eyes to
see. However, there are other critical judgments to reckon
with prior to or during the judgments that occur during the
Tribulation. Let's look at them.

1. *Judgment of the believer's sin.* "Without shedding of
   blood is no remission" of sin (Hebrews 9:22). More
   than nineteen hundred years ago, Christ came from
   heaven's glory to shed His precious blood for a world
   of ungodly sinners. He did not die for His own sin, for
   He knew no sin, but became sin for us (2 Corinthians
   5:21). Through His substitutionary death, dying for

mankind, all who receive this Christ can have the past, present, and future stains of sin forgiven and forgotten (Hebrews 8:12). "The blood of Jesus Christ [God's] Son cleanseth us from all sin" (1 John 1:7; see Titus 3:5 and Romans 8:1).

2. *Judgment of the believer's service.* The believer's lifetime of works are judged at the bema seat (2 Corinthians 5:10). Some Christians do not take this judgment seriously. However, to do so is to refuse life in accordance with God's plan. The life of a Christian will be judged, and God's pronouncement of that verdict must not be taken lightly. If one fails God's investigative judgment in that day, there will be no crowns to place before Christ on His throne (Revelation 4:10-11).

3. *Judgment of Israel.* When the armies of the world converge on the Middle East, culminating at Israel (Zechariah 14:2; Ezekiel 38, 39), this period of bloody devastation becomes the Time of Jacob's Trouble (Jeremiah 30:7). During this Tribulation period, the whole world will come into judgment. One in three will be consumed by fire, and one-half of all people will die during this time (Revelation 6:8; 9:18). Numerous passages describe this time as the earth's worst event (Jeremiah 30:7; Daniel 12:1; Joel 2:2). Jesus said, "Then shall be great tribulation, such as was not since the beginning of the world to this time, no, nor ever shall be" (Matthew 24:21). At this time they will "look on Him whom they have pierced." Their response will cause them to repent and recognize Christ as Messiah.

4. *Judgment of the nations.* Matthew 25 pictures the glorious return of Christ to this earth. This correlates

with Revelation 19:11-16 when Christ returns as King of kings and Lord of lords. After Armageddon—and before He establishes His millennial kingdom upon earth (Revelation 20:4)—Christ purges the earth of its rebels. The "sheep" nations are invited to enter the kingdom (Millennium) along with the "brethren," the Jews. The *goats*—those who mistreated Jews and rejected Christ—are cast into the Lake of Fire (Matthew 25:41,46).

Twenty-One Special Judgments

There are a total of twenty-one special judgments that fall upon earth during the Tribulation period. They are in three series of sevens described as seals, trumpets, and vials (or bowls):

The Seal Judgments: This is the beginning of the program of God to pour out judgments upon the earth. I encourage you to open your Bible and read each judgment carefully to understand the finality of God's pronouncements. These include:

1. The world's greatest dictator (Revelation 6:1-2)

2. The world's greatest war (Revelation 6:3-4)

3. The world's greatest famine (Revelation 6:5-6)

4. The world's greatest death blow (Revelation 6:7-8)

5. The world's greatest persecution (Revelation 6:9-11)

6. The world's greatest ecological disaster (Revelation 6:12-17)

7. The world's greatest hour of fear ... actually the lull before the storm (Revelation 8:1)

The Trumpet Judgments: The trumpets of heaven sound an alarm throughout the world announcing the public judgments of God. Each blast ushers in an added judgment.

8. The world's greatest fire (Revelation 8:7)

9. The world's greatest oceanic disturbance (Revelation 8:8-9)

10. The world's greatest pollution of water (Revelation 8:10-11)

11. The world's greatest darkness (Revelation 8:12-13)

12. The world's greatest pestilential invasion (Revelation 9:1-6)

13. The world's greatest army (Revelation 9:16)

14. The world's greatest storm (Revelation 11:15-19)

The Vial Judgments:

15. The world's greatest epidemic (Revelation 16:2)

16. The world's greatest contamination by blood (Revelation 16:3-7)

17. The world's greatest contamination by blood, continued (Revelation 16:3-7)

18. The world's greatest scorching (Revelation 16:8-9)

19. The world's greatest plague (Revelation 16:10-11)

20. The world's greatest invasion (Revelation 16:12)

21. The world's greatest earthquake (Revelation 16:18)

These twenty-one judgments unleash unbelievable war, ecological disasters, and atomic catastrophe on our earth. Note this judgment in particular; Revelation 14:20 reads,

Question 16

"And the winepress was trodden without the city, and blood came out of the winepress, even unto the horse bridles, by the space of a thousand and six hundred furlongs." According to today's calculations, that is a river of blood two hundred miles long—*the exact length of the nation of Israel.* Think of it! An entire nation saturated and soaked with blood. As believers, you and I can be grateful that the Rapture is coming, because it means we—the Church of Jesus Christ—will not be present to endure this terrible suffering. The Bride will be at home, at the marriage ceremony, and afterward return for the supper (Revelation 19:7-16).

What a wonderful and, gracious God we have, who will use the very wrath of the tribulation as an instrument to prepare for the glories of the millennium.[1]

H. L. Willmington, The King Is Coming

Question 17

What is Jacob's Time of Trouble?

In Jeremiah 30:7-8 we read, "Alas! for that day is great, so that none is like it: it is even the time of Jacob's trouble; but he shall be saved out of it. For it shall come to pass in that day, saith the LORD of hosts, that I will break his yoke from off thy neck, and will burst thy bonds, and strangers shall no more serve themselves of him." Jacob is Israel. This is reconfirmed in Romans 11:26: "And so all Israel shall be saved: as it is written, There shall come out of Sion the Deliverer, and shall turn away ungodliness from Jacob." This period of time is also referred to as "Daniel's Seventieth Week" (Daniel 9:24).

In biblical history, the first sixty-nine weeks refer exclusively to Israel and, as we've noted earlier, it follows logically that the seventieth or final week must also involve the nation of Israel. A careful survey of chapters 30 and 31 of Jeremiah summarizes Israel's endurance in the hour of Tribulation—a truth affirmed by all the Old Testament prophets. In Ezekiel 38 and 39, eighteen different passages mark Israel as the victim of Gog and Magog's deadliest war. Jacob's trouble is so named because of Jeremiah's prophecy;

"Alas! for that day is great, so that none is like it: it is even the time of Jacob's trouble," and Jacob is Israel (2 Kings 17:34). Here the prophet was speaking of the seven-year period known as the Tribulation when, after the removal of the Church, earth suddenly plunges into its most horrendous hour (Matthew 24:21).

A further word on the seventieth week of Daniel—a chapter on which a full understanding of the end times rests. This significant "week" will be a period of 7 years, 84 months, each having 360 days by the old Jewish calendar, for a total of 2,520 days. In Revelation 11:3 and Revelation 12:6, half of this period is recorded as 1,260 days. When that is doubled, it becomes 2,520 days. It is a time of unprecedented trouble. "Alas! for that day is great, so that none is like it" (Jeremiah 30:7).

This period is divided into three sections. The *first division* comprised 7 weeks, or a period of 49 years, and had to do with the rebuilding of Jerusalem in troublesome times past (Daniel 9:25). The *second division* of 62 weeks, or 434 years, signaled the time of Christ's death after the rebuilding of Jerusalem. This prophecy was fulfilled exactly on schedule when Christ came and offered Himself to Israel, but was rejected and cut off (Daniel 9:26). This was the Crucifixion, after the completion of His offer as King. The rebuilding of Jerusalem began on March 14, 445 B.C., and Christ was cut off on schedule. Now Israel must pay the price for rejecting her King. So *a final week is coming* when the Antichrist will confirm his peace covenant with many for one week, or seven years (Daniel 9:27). When the Antichrist usurps the throne that rightfully belongs to Christ, he shall destroy the city and the sanctuary; "and the end thereof shall be with a flood, and unto the end of the war desolations are determined" (Daniel 9:26). This is the time of Jacob's (or Israel's) trouble, resulting from the rejection of Christ. God's chastisement then creates an attitude of acceptance for the true King—the Lord Jesus Christ—at the close of the seventieth week.

There is no doubt about it; Israel travails greatly before the King returns. Jeremiah's prophecy proves it: "For, lo, the days come, saith the LORD, that I will bring again the captivity of my people Israel and Judah, saith the LORD; and I will cause them to return to the land that I gave to their fathers, and they shall possess it. And these are the words that the LORD spake concerning Israel and concerning Judah. For thus saith the LORD; We have heard a voice of trembling, of fear, and not of peace. Ask ye now, and see whether a man doth travail with child? wherefore do I see every man with his hands on his loins, as a woman in travail, and all faces are turned into paleness? Alas! for that day is great, so that none is like it: it is even the time of Jacob's trouble" (Jeremiah 30:3-7).

Daniel also describes the day of sorrow when a monstrous anti-Semite dictator, satanically energized, "shall speak great words against the most High, and shall wear out the saints of the most High" (Daniel 7:25). The Lord Jesus Himself stated in Matthew 24:9, 21-22, "Then shall they deliver you up to be afflicted, and shall kill you: and ye shall be hated of all nations for my name's sake.... For then shall be great tribulation, such as was not since the beginning of the world to this time, no, nor ever shall be. And except those days should be shortened, there should no flesh be saved: but for the elect's [Israel's] sake those days shall be shortened."

Behold, thou shalt conceive in thy womb, and bring forth a son, and shalt call his name Jesus. He shall be great, and shall be called the Son of the Highest: and the Lord God shall give unto him the throne of his father David: And he shall reign over the house of Jacob for ever; and of his kingdom there shall be no end.

Luke 1:31-33

Question 18

Some have said that Israel herself is a sign.
What does this mean? What is the significance
of the "regathering" of Israel?

The Jew himself is God's timepiece and the key that unlocks every door of prophecy. This is because God has a special love for Israel. Deuteronomy 7:6-8 declares, "For thou art an holy people unto the LORD thy God: the LORD thy God hath chosen thee to be a special people unto himself, above all people that are upon the face of the earth. The LORD did not set his love upon you, nor choose you, because ye were more in number than any people; for ye were the fewest of all people: But because the LORD loved you." God chose Israel "to be a peculiar people unto himself, above all the nations that are upon the earth" (Deuteronomy 14:2). This is the first great insight I want you to grasp—*that God chose the people of Israel simply because He loved them.* No more, no less. David was so enraptured with the truth of God's love for Israel that he exclaimed in 1 Chronicles 17:22, "For thy people Israel didst thou make thine own people for ever; and thou, LORD, becamest their God." As we progress with this question, it will become abundantly clear why to this day Israel itself is a major sign of Christ's imminent return.

The Great Escape

The Lord God Jehovah told the people of Israel that their country was to be located "in the midst of the land" (Ezekiel 38:12), or more literally, in the "navel of the earth." Its capital city, Jerusalem, was to be situated in the center of the nations (Ezekiel 5:5); and in that capital city the Lord was to put His name forever, and forever, declaring that His eye and His heart would be there perpetually (1 Kings 9:3). There the Lord promised to establish the throne of David forever (2 Samuel 7:16) and finally to give that throne to His own divine and eternal Son. Luke 1:31-33 states, "Behold, thou shalt conceive in thy womb, and bring forth a son, and shalt call his name JESUS. He shall be great, and shall be called the Son of the Highest: and the Lord God shall give unto him the throne of his father David: And he shall reign over the house of Jacob for ever; and of his kingdom there shall be no end." Are you beginning to see how much God loved Israel and its people? However, it was not all love, sweetness, and light.

God also warned the children of Israel of an imminent worldwide dispersion if they thumbed their noses at Him in disobedience. He went so far as to tell them that His Son would delay His rule if their hearts became wicked and hardened. To see if God is a God of His word, let us look at the prophetical utterances to see if they really took place. Scripture tells us that Israel was, in fact, driven out of its land and scattered among the nations of the earth because of its widespread disobedience. During this world-wide dispersion, God visited the Gentiles, "to take out of them a people for his name" (Acts 15:14). In the meantime, Israel existed many days without a king, without a prince, without a sacrifice, without an image, without an ephod (a sacred garment of gold, blue, purple, scarlet, and fine twined linen worn by the priest), and without teraphim (Hosea 3:4). Devout religious Jews cry vehemently at the Wailing Wall in Jerusalem because they have been without all of these things for centuries—just as God declared they would be without them. Since all these prophecies have come to pass according to prophetical utterance, and since God has shown His mighty power in bringing each utterance to fulfillment, let us now consider the predictions in upcoming questions and answers to see if His coming is near.

The Regathering of Israel

The second part of the question is, "What is the significance of the 'regathering' of Israel?" Scores of Bible passages clearly indicate that the reestablishment of Israel in its ancient homeland will take place when Messiah is ready to return to earth. The Messiah is none other than the Lord Jesus Christ of Luke 1:32. Deuteronomy 30:3 states, "The LORD thy God will. . . return and gather thee from all the nations, whither the LORD thy God hath scattered thee." In similar language, Isaiah 11:12 tells us, "And he shall set up an ensign for the nations, and shall assemble the outcasts of Israel, and gather together the dispersed of Judah from the four corners of the earth." Again, Acts 15:16 declares, "After this." After what? Look at verse 14: God "did visit the Gentiles, to take out of them a people for his name." This has been occurring since Cornelius, the first Gentile convert, received Christ in Acts 10. God says, "After this [after the Gentiles have had their opportunity] I will return, and will build again the tabernacle of David, which is fallen down; and I will build again the ruins thereof, and I will set it up" (Acts 15:16).

An important historical note: In A.D. 70, Titus the Roman general smashed Jerusalem and drove the Jews into their dispersion. This is called "the diaspora," or worldwide dispersion of the Jews. From that hour until 1948, the Jews had no homeland to call their own. Instead, the nations of the world hated them, mistreated them, and labeled them, as we noted earlier, "wandering Jews." God, however, said that He would bring His people back to their own land and that this regathering would happen near the time when Messiah would set up His kingdom on earth: "And I will plant [Israel] upon their land, and they shall no more be pulled up out of their land which I have given them, saith the LORD thy God" (Amos 9:15).

God has put the Jews in their land to stay forever. Is it not interesting that the Arab nations refused to recognize Israel when it became a nation in 1948? The Arabs were determined to drive Israel into the sea and obliterate her memory from the face of the earth. However, God had other—and better—plans and, in the end, God's way always wins the day. He said in the verse just quoted that Israel would remain in its land forever after He planted the nation there. Therefore, in 1974 the Egyptians, Syrians, and others negotiated with Israel, recognizing for the first time that Israel was indeed a nation and *in* its land to stay. Have you studied the extraordinary message in Ezekiel 37, which alludes to this event, and which further describes the prophet's vision of the dry bones? Here is a portion of this amazing passage:

The hand of the LORD was upon me, and carried me out in the spirit of the LORD, and set me down in the midst of the valley which was full of bones. And caused me to pass by them round about: and, behold, there were very many in the open valley; and, lo, they were very dry. And he said unto me, Son of man, can these bones live? And I answered, O Lord GOD, thou knowest. Again he said unto me. Prophesy upon these bones, and say unto them, O ye dry bones, hear the word of the LORD. Thus saith the Lord GOD unto these bones; Behold, I will cause breath to enter into you, and ye shall live: And I will lay sinews upon you, and will bring up flesh upon you, and cover you with skin, and put breath in you, and ye shall live; and ye shall know that I am the LORD. So I prophesied as I was commanded: and as I prophesied, there was a noise, and behold a shaking, and the bones came together, bone to his bone. And when I beheld, lo, the sinews and the flesh came up upon them, and the skin covered them above: but there was no breath in them. Then said he unto me, Prophesy unto the wind, prophesy, son of man, and say to the wind. Thus saith the Lord GOD; Come from the four winds, O breath, and breathe upon these slain, that they may live. So I prophesied as he commanded me, and the breath came into them, and they lived, and stood up upon their feet, an exceeding great army. Then he said unto me, Son of man, these bones are the whole house of Israel: behold, they say, Our bones are dried, and our hope is lost: we are cut off for our parts. Therefore prophesy and say unto them. Thus saith the Lord GOD; Behold, O my people, I will open your graves [Gentile nations], and cause you to come up out of your graves [the Gentile nations], and bring you into the land of Israel. (Ezekiel 37:1-12)

There is no secret here. Verse 11 proclaims: "These bones are the whole house of Israel." In 1948, the Jews put up a flag—the six-pointed Star of David. After being scattered throughout the earth for nearly nineteen hundred years, they had finally become a nation! The current population of Israel is more than five million—consisting of Jews who have returned from 120 nations of the world, speaking more than eighty-three languages. While in Israel, I spoke to a Jew who had recently returned from Spanish Morocco. As I sat with him on a bus going from Arab Israel to another part of the country, we talked about the black Jews who were just then returning to Israel from Ethiopia. He quickly said, "Yes, we have come from all nations." When the Ethiopian Jews left Jerusalem nineteen hundred years ago, they said, "We will never go back to our homeland until it is time for Messiah to return." Today these Jews from Ethiopia—called Falashas—have returned in massive numbers. They have also come from Russia and Ukraine—the final sign (see Jeremiah 3:17-18). For these reasons alone, I can say with full conviction—and trust you can also—that Jesus Christ's return to this earth is near, even at the door.

And they shall fall by the edge of the sword, and shall be led away captive into all nations: and Jerusalem shall be trodden down of the Gentiles, until the times of the Gentiles be fulfilled. And there shall be signs in the sun, and in the moon, and in the stars', and upon the earth distress of nations, with perplexity; the sea and the waves roaring.

Luke 21:24-25

Question 19

Jerusalem has always been under the heel of the Gentiles. When will ownership of Jerusalem return to the Jews; And when will the Tribulation period untimately fall on unbelievers?

We find further dramatic signs of Christ's return in Luke 21:24 - 28. Jesus said: "And they shall fall by the edge of the sword, and shall be led away captive into all nations: and Jerusalem shall be trodden down of the Gentiles, until the times of the Gentiles be fulfilled. And there shall be signs in the sun, and in the moon, and in the stars; and upon the earth distress of nations, with perplexity; the sea and the waves roaring; Men's hearts failing them for fear, and for looking after those things which are coming on the earth: for the powers of heaven shall be shaken. And then shall they see the Son of man coming in a cloud with power and great glory. And when these things begin to come to pass, then look up, and lift up your heads; for your redemption draweth nigh."

This portion of Scripture pinpoints the time of Christ's statement in utmost simplicity. In modern grammar, the Savior declares, "There is an hour coming when My people, the Jews, shall control Jerusalem. At this moment of time, there shall also be signs in space coupled with a trouble-filled world. When all of these events occur simultaneously, look up because My return to earth is very near." Jerusalem had been under the heel of the Gentiles. In fact, the Gentiles controlled the city for twenty-five centuries, but in our lifetime a miracle happened. Jerusalem was captured by the Jews in a six-day war fought June 5-10, 1967—one of the most important signs ever concerning Christ's return predicted in Luke 21:24. But there's more. Jesus added in verse 25 that signs would occur in the sun, moon, and stars. Think of this. Twenty-five months after Jerusalem was captured by the Jews, June of 1967, Neil Armstrong stepped on the moon in July of 1969. Coincidence? Hardly.

Signs of Judgment by Fire

As we have already learned, the period of time that follows the Rapture and precedes Christ's return to earth is called the Tribulation (Revelation 7:14). The Rapture is described in Revelation 4:1 and the Revelation—Christ's return to earth to receive His church in Revelation 19:11. The chapters between the two events constitute the Tribulation Hour—a seven-year period of judgment. Christ referred to this period in the statement, "As it was in the days of Lot... Even thus shall it be in the day when the Son of man is revealed" (Luke 17:28, 30). The fire that burned Sodom and Gomorrah was all-consuming—the result of wickedness and of turning a deaf ear to the Almighty. Bad as it was for Sodom and Gomorrah, their fate is nothing compared to the coming human devastation that will afflict the people of earth during the Tribulation Hour. Jeremiah 30:7 declares, "Alas! for that day is great, so that none is like it." Daniel 12:1 states, "There shall be a time of trouble, such as never was since there was a nation." Jesus also declared in

Matthew 24:21, "For then shall be great tribulation, such as was not since the beginning of the world to this time, no, nor ever shall be." Included in this horrendous portrayal is a world on fire— similar to the judgment of Lot's day. The Bible says, "The flaming flame shall not be quenched" (Ezekiel 20:47). Again, "The whole land shall be devoured by the fire of his jealousy" (Zephaniah 1:18). "For, behold, the day cometh, that shall burn as an oven" (Malachi 4:1). "And the third part of trees was burnt up, and all green grass was burnt up" (Revelation 8:7). "By these three was the third part of men killed, by the fire, and by the smoke, and by the brimstone" (Revelation 9:18).

A stockpile of nuclear explosives jams the weapons arsenals of the world today. Reports indicate that the amount is equivalent to one ton of TNT for every person alive. Think of the mass devastation that shall be unleashed on this world during the Tribulation Hour! But God's people will escape this catastrophic judgment. Revelation 3:10 declares, "I also will keep thee from [*ek*—out of] the hour of temptation, which shall come upon all the world, to try them that dwell upon the earth."

And the word of the Lord came unto me, saying,
Son of man, set thy face against Gog, the land of Magog,
the chief prince of Meshech and Tubal,
and prophesy against him.

Ezekiel 38:1-2

Question 20

Will Russia invade Israel?
If so, under what circumstances?
Also, clarify the importance of the
Israeli capture of Jerusalem in 1967.

O ne of the most significant prophecies about the
Middle East and the Rapture of the Church concerns Russia's imminent invasion of Israel. In the
previous question, we addressed the issue of Israel becoming a nation. Why is that reality so vital to our discussion?
Because eighteen times in Ezekiel 38-39, the prophet states
that Russia will wage war against Israel. *For nearly nineteen
hundred years, there was no nation called Israel*—thus
no government and no specific piece of Middle East real
estate that the Jews of the diaspora could call their own.
Now you and I have lived to see Israel become a mighty
nation, a people to be reckoned with in the commonwealth
of nations. Therefore, when God's Word foretells a Russian
invasion of Israel, and we know that such a nation now
exists, we can only assume that the coming of the Lord
must be near. Ezekiel 38:1-2 states, "And the word of the
LORD came unto me, saying, Son of man, set thy face against
Gog, the land of Magog, the chief prince of Meshech and
Tubal, and prophesy against him." Since we will study these
names in detail later, I will not spend time attempting to

prove that this refers to Russia. I simply want you to see, for
now, that this is a northern enemy, for they come from the
north (see Ezekiel 38:15; 39:2). Remember, Russia is due
north of Israel. If one draws a line northward from Israel,
he passes directly through Moscow. As this great end-time
invasion begins, they will come against the mountains of
Israel (Ezekiel 38:8). Verse 16 says, "Thou shalt come up
against my people of Israel." Verse 19: "Surely in that day
there shall be a great shaking in the land of Israel." Ezekiel
39:2 says, "I will turn thee back, and leave but the sixth
part of thee, and will cause thee to come up from the north
parts, and will bring thee upon the mountains of Israel."
Verse 4: "Thou shalt fall upon the mountains of Israel."
Verse 12: "And seven months shall the house of Israel be
burying of them."

Let me repeat that Russia's invasion of Israel could not
occur until Israel became a nation. *There was no such nation, for two thousand years, until 1948.* Thus, this event
could not have occurred in times past. However, since Israel
now exists as a viable, powerful nation (and has recaptured
Jerusalem after twenty-five hundred years of dominance
by Gentiles), and because Russia will move against Israel
only when *she is a nation,* here is the thrilling scenario
to follow—something that is already beginning to happen
in front of our eyes today. Follow me closely. Ezekiel 36
and 37 describe the Jew returning to his own land and setting up his government. This occurred in 1948. In Ezekiel
chapters 40-48, Messiah is back on earth—and that is when
you and I have returned with Him to rule and reign for
one thousand years (Revelation 20:4). Between Israel's becoming a nation—which you and I have lived to see—and
Messiah's return to earth, a war with Russia takes place

in the Middle East (read Ezekiel 38 and 39). The Jews are now home. Today Israel has its own government, monetary system, and well-fortified and -trained armed forces. Russia marches when Israel is a nation, followed by Messiah's return. There is no doubt that we are living at the very edge of this hour when the sign concerning Russia's march to the Middle East is about to be fulfilled. It could happen at any moment, followed by Christ's return. This ancient Jewish teaching is found in *Avoda Zara* 3B. The clock is ticking toward midnight. Jesus is coming again, and the day of His return is at hand.

What Is the Importance of the Jews Finally Reclaiming Jerusalem?

Since 400 B.C. the city of Jerusalem has been handed over to one Gentile superpower after another. Here are a few of those "transference" dates since A.D. 70 concerning Jerusalem: A.D. 70, the Romans; 614, the Persians; 637, Caliph Omar; 1099, the Crusaders; 1187, Saladin; 1250, the Egyptian Mamelukes; 1517, the Turks; 1917, the British; and finally, in 1967, the Jews captured Jerusalem. The event took place during the Six-Day War, from June 5 to 10 of that year, The Jewish control of Jerusalem *is a most important sign* because of Jesus' statement in Luke 21:24. The disciples had asked Him, "When are you going to return to this earth?" Jesus replied, "[Jerusalem] shall fall by the edge of the sword, and shall be led away captive into all nations: and Jerusalem shall be trodden down of the Gentiles, until the times of the Gentiles be fulfilled." What was the Savior saying? Simply that the Jews would be scattered throughout the world and the city of Jerusalem controlled by Gentile powers until the time of His return. All the various Gentile groups—the Romans, the Persians, the Crusaders, the Egyptians, the Turks, and the English—controlled Jerusalem from A.D. 70 until May 1967.

Then, in June 1967 the Jews took control of Jerusalem for the first time in more than nineteen hundred years. When we tie this historical information to Ezekiel's bones coming to life, the Jews returning from the Gentile nations, and the earlier prophecies already outlined, there can be only one conclusion: Christ must come to earth soon, primarily because during the third and final invasion of the Armageddon campaign, all nations come against Jerusalem to battle and to take it back from the Jews (Zechariah 14:2). This would have been impossible before 1967 since the Jewish people did not possess Jerusalem until that Six-Day War fought June 5-10, 1967. Thus, when the final invasion during Armageddon occurs, Christ descends to the Mount of Olives to end the atrocities committed against Israel at Jerusalem and to then set up His kingdom (Zechariah 14:4).

For then shall be great tribulation, such as was not
since the beginning of the world to this time,
no, nor ever shall be.

Matthew 24:21

Question 21

What signs exist in Israel today that provide clues to a rapidly approaching Tribulation period?

O f the hundreds of questions I am asked, issues re-
lated to the Great Tribulation always seem to top
the list. To review, there is going to be a terrible
period of tribulation. Jeremiah 30:7 says, "Alas! for that day
is great, so that none is like it." Daniel 12:1 warns, "There
shall be a time of trouble, such as never was since there
was a nation," and Jesus Himself said in Matthew 24:21,
"For then shall be great tribulation, such as was not since
the beginning of the world to this time, no, nor ever shall
be." Although this event will not be the end of the world, it
will bring death to one-half of our planet's inhabitants: "By
these three was the third part of men killed, by the fire,
and by the smoke, and by the brimstone" (Revelation 9:18).
When one combines the cumulative facts and figures from
the Book of Revelation in 9:18 and 6:8, he discovers that
nearly one-half of the earth's population will be destroyed
in the greatest fiery conflagration and pestilential judgment
that have ever occurred in the history of mankind.

Again, however, let me remind you: This great war
signals the coming of Jesus Christ to the earth, when He

reveals Himself to the entire world and stops the carnage (Revelation 11:18). As we learned earlier, *this event is called the Revelation,* and it is the second phase of the Second Coming. We have also learned that prior to the Revelation, a Rapture—the evacuation of all saints, dead and living, from the earth—will occur (Revelation 4:1). Immediately following the Rapture, the Tribulation Hour, that period of seven years of unprecedented turmoil and trouble, begins. Then, at the end of the seven years, Jesus Christ comes back to the earth to set up His kingdom for a thousand years—called the Millennium.

Remember that all the signs of Matthew 24, Mark 13, and Luke 17 and 21 point directly to the second phase of the Second Coming, and not to the Rapture. If there were not one sign in existence anywhere at this moment, we could still go home to be with our Lord, because all the signs could occur during the seven-year period described in chapters 6-18 of the Book of Revelation. However, since all the signs point to Christ's return to the earth—not His coming in the clouds (Revelation 4:1) but His coming to the earth (Revelation 19:11), and since you and I as Christians return with Him to the earth—then every sign in Revelation 6-18 points to our coming back to the earth as well. This glorious event must occur soon since all signs are already in place.

Three Signs in Israel

For many decades. Orthodox Jewish rabbis said: "When three signs appear in the Holy Land, it will be the hour for Messiah to return." What are these three signs?

1. Horseless carriages, or modern automobiles, running

through the streets of Jerusalem.

2. Jerusalem being defended by airplanes.

3. The desert of Israel blossoming as a rose.

Have these things happened? I will leave the answers to you. When my wife, Rexella, and I last visited the Holy Land, we had an opportunity to preach, teach, and spend time with Jewish Christians in Jerusalem. So what I am about to share with you regarding the "signs in Israel" is not theoretical. As I began to observe them, I said, "Rexella, these are the signs that point to our return with Jesus Christ." Since they are already in progress and are now being fulfilled, Jesus must be coming soon for His church in that glorious event called the Rapture. Let's investigate these three signs that the rabbis have so long awaited.

Nahum 2:3-4 states, "The chariots shall be with flaming torches in the day of his [Messiah's] preparation. . . . The chariots shall rage in the streets, they shall justle one against another [accidents] in the broad ways: they shall seem like torches [headlights and taillights], they shall run like the lightnings [the speed of these vehicles running through the streets of Jerusalem]." This phenomenon is presently occurring!

Isaiah 31:5 tells us, "As birds flying, so will the LORD of hosts defend Jerusalem." Since A.D. 70 the much beleaguered city of Jerusalem has passed from one Gentile power to another. In 1517, the Turks took control and maintained their authority for exactly four hundred years. Then, in 1917, General Allenby of England marched into Jerusalem with his troops. The British had just discovered airplanes, and as they flew overhead, the Turks, never having seen such machines, became frightened, dropped their guns, and fled the city. Britain's conquest of Jerusalem was one of the few battles in history won without weapons. Why? *Because the Turks saw men flying as birds over Jerusalem.* This event was the beginning of the fulfillment of Isaiah's prophecy. Today, as one stands anywhere in the Holy Land, he sees jets flying overhead daily. There is no end to it. The prophecy is here. It is being fulfilled *now!*

Isaiah 35:1 promises, "The desert shall rejoice, and blossom as the rose." During our first visit to the Holy Land Rexella and I noticed that everywhere we looked the ground was dry, arid, barren, rocky, and mountainous. Today, however, when one visits the Holy Land, it is anything but arid. It has been wondrously transformed into hundreds of square miles of fertile, blooming, productive land. Truly, Isaiah's promise has become a reality; the third major sign pointing to Messiah's coming.

But as the days of Noah were, so shall also the coming of the Son of man be. For as in the days that were before the flood they were eating and drinking, marrying and giving in marriage, until the day that Noah entered into the ark. And knew not until the flood came, and took them all away; so shall also the coming of the Son of man be.

Matthew 24:37-39

Question 22

What role will mankind itself play in ushering in the end of the age?

Signs Concerning Mankind

In describing the attitude of mankind and the conditions that will prevail upon the earth at the time of Christ's return, the Lord Jesus said: "But as the days of Noah were, so shall also the coming of the Son of man be. For as in the days that were before the flood they were eating and drinking, marrying and giving in marriage, until the day that Noah entered into the ark, And knew not until the flood came, and took them all away; so shall also the coming of the Son of man be. Then shall two be in the field; the one shall be taken, and the other left. Two women shall be grinding at the mill; the one shall be taken, and the other left. Watch therefore: for ye know not what hour your Lord doth come" (Matthew 24:37-42).

In this portion of Scripture we discover that, upon Christ's return, conditions on earth will be exactly as they were during Noah's era: "And it came to pass, when men began to multiply on the face of the earth, and daughters were born unto them, that the sons of God saw the daughters of men that they were fair; and they took them wives of all which they chose.... And God saw that the wickedness of man was great in the earth, and that every imagination of the thoughts of his heart was only evil continually.... The earth also was corrupt before God, and the earth was filled with violence" (Genesis 6:1-2,5,11). Would you not agree this passage is as current as this morning's headlines?

Sex Outside of Marriage

The first sign in this listing has to do with sex. "They took them wives" (Genesis 6:2). In doing this, they went against the lesson God had given them at creation. God said, "It is not good that the man should be alone; I will make him an help meet for him" (Genesis 2:18-). What did God create? He did not create a man for a man. Instead, He created one woman for one man. This is God's established order for the universe. Lust and sin have, however, kicked a dent in the Almighty's program. Men and women today are running away from one another, leaving children destitute and homes broken. Why? Because their number one concern is the satisfaction of their own flesh. Someone compliments them, they become enamored, and suddenly they find themselves infatuated with the *idea of love* rather than the genuine article. Soon they go through a predictable pattern of adultery, divorce, and remarriage, only to discover that their second and third choices were not much better than the first. The trouble was not their first mate, but sin. Naturally, there are exceptions. Today, approximately half of all American marriages end up on the casualty list. The signs of Noah's era are all around us. It is one more example that the Rapture is near.

Jesus further added that they were "giving in marriage." Dr, M. R. DeHaan and other scholars render this as "exchanging mates" or "wife swapping." Swingers are still the rage of the day—and in many communities where you might not expect such unsavory activity. Couples get together for a supper bash and end up exchanging their mates for a night of glorified orgies. How low can humans go? The situation dominates modern society, and it has the curse of God upon it. We also see millions today shacking up and living together without a marriage license, and the pulpits remain silent. Hebrews 13:4 states, "Marriage is honourable in all, and the bed undefiled: but whoremongers and adulterers God will judge." Still, despite God's warning, millions disobey His commandments. They live life loosely and laugh off the consequences. Sin, however; offers its own reward, and its wages are always death (Romans 6:23). The day of sifting and judgment is coming. Soon a sin-crazy, hellbent generation will meet the God of holiness: The string will snap and the joke will end.

Gluttony and Drunkenness

Christ also mentioned gluttony and drunkenness as signs foreshadowing His return. He said, "They were eating and drinking . . . until the day that Noah entered into the ark, And knew not [believed not] until the flood came, and took them all away; so shall also the coming of the Son of man be" (Matthew 24:38-39). The fool's motto has not changed over the centuries, "Eat, drink, and be merry, for tomorrow we die." Bars and nightclubs throughout the nation advertise a "happy hour," or an "attitude-adjustment hour," meaning that drinks go for half-price during a specified time. But what does this really mean? That one can choose an eternity without Christ at discounted prices. Never have we had so many alcoholics and drug addicts. America's combined total of addicts exceeds twenty million. Europe, Asia, and all the continents of the world are in the same dilemma. Satan's brew is eye-enticing and nose-appealing. Millions have fallen victim to his seduction. However, it will not last forever. The third and fourth seals of the Apocalypse picture shortages, poverty, hunger, and death.

Revelation 6:7-8 states, "And when he had opened the fourth seal, I heard the voice of the fourth beast say, Come and see. And I looked, and behold a pale horse: and his name that sat on him was Death, and Hell followed with him. And power was given unto them over the fourth part of the earth, to kill with sword, and with hunger, and with death, and with the beasts of the earth." When life ends, as it must for all mortals, because "it is appointed unto men once to die" (Hebrews 9:27), the sinner must enter a place where even water is unattainable. Christ told of a lost sinner crying out from hell, saying, "Send Lazarus, that he may dip the tip of his finger in water, and cool my tongue; for I am tormented in this flame" (Luke 16:24). Liquor is not worth such eternal thirst. The Holy Spirit declares in 1 Corinthians 6:9-10, "Know ye not that the unrighteous shall not inherit the kingdom of God? Be not deceived: neither fornicators, nor idolaters, nor adulterers, nor effeminate, nor abusers of themselves with mankind, Nor thieves, nor covetous, nor drunkards, nor revilers, nor extortioners, shall inherit the kingdom of God." Galatians 5:19-21 mentions seventeen sins, and the sixteenth is listed as "drunkenness," which brings eternal loss, for the conclusion of the text states, "They which do such things shall not inherit the kingdom of God." Do not let sin rob you of being caught up with Christ in that glorious day that is soon to come.

Cry aloud, spare not, lift up thy voice like a trumpet, and shew my people their transgression, and the house of Jacob their sins.

Isaiah 58:1

Question 23

Is it my imagination, or are corruption and violence on the increase? What does this have to do with Christ's return?

Corruption

Noah's era was also one of corruption: "Every imagination of the thoughts of [mankind's] heart was only evil continually" (Genesis 6:5). The result: "The earth also was corrupt before God" (Genesis 6:11). It takes no stretch of a person's imagination to see a world of men filled with vile imaginations. This is history's worst hour. Filthy pornographic magazines and X-rated movies have brainwashed the depraved into submission. Vile, lewd, and licentious pornography floods the world. Savages are roaming the streets raping and sodomizing victims. Since morality is the essence of God's Ten Commandments, as well as the entire teaching of the Holy Bible, Christians should be crusaders in the battle against the world, the flesh, and the devil. How does it make you feel to see pornographic bookstores within a few doors of gospel-preaching churches? Unfortunately, many believers are doing nothing to stop this intrusion on our morality. This is contrary to the Almighty God who demands that His servants "Cry aloud, spare not, lift up thy voice like a trumpet, and shew my people their transgression, and the house of Jacob their sins" (Isaiah 58:1).

If we do not want kiddy porn and its sister, prostitution, to arrive in our communities, we must rid ourselves of obscenity at every level or eventually it will touch the innocent lives of our children. Even the Supreme Court has stated emphatically that the first amendment does not protect obscenity. The laws must be enforced at all levels: local, state, and federal. Many Christians think their children are safe because they are in a Christian school and church. Nothing could be further from the truth. Our homes are being invaded by television filth from morning to night, with the afternoon "freak shows" walking away with the ratings! Yet, millions of American Christians have accepted the philosophy that there is no right or wrong. The result of our inaction? Purveyors of smut capitalize on the opportunities that an uncaring public hands them on a silver platter. The present scene has become so nauseating that celebrities, professional counselors, and media executives themselves are speaking out. One famous comedian, Steve Alien, declared publicly that television has gotten too dirty and that the networks televise junk just to keep the ratings high. A broadcasting executive asked his industry this probing question, "Have we sunk so low that we have sold our children to the dogs in order to make a dollar?"

You've probably seen the popular armbands worn by many Christians—young and old alike. There are only four letters on the band: WWJD—a question and a reminder to the wearer: *What Would Jesus Do?* Good question. "What *would* Jesus do? Well, I can tell you one thing He's going to do: *He's going to return in majesty and glory.* He's going to remove His church from the porn, the permissiveness, and the poverty of morality and arrange for His bride to meet Him in the air in a sky-splitting event known as the Rapture. While we remain on planet earth, you and I must heed the apostle's words, "For we wrestle not against flesh and blood, but against principalities, against powers, against the rulers of the darkness of this world, against spiritual wickedness in high places" (Ephesians 6:12). This bombardment of continual wickedness, implanting so much filth and false values in our collective minds, is presently reaping an abundant harvest morally, spiritually, and socially. Just as the degenerated values of society in Noah's day filled the world with violence, so sin, crime, and fear stalk humanity as we come to the close of the twentieth century.

I'm confident this situation will continue to deteriorate because the sign will break forth in all its debauchery during the Tribulation Hour. *We are already observing the preview of coming events.* Life will not be worth living during the Tribulation, because Satan will be cast out of the heavens and will be enthroned upon the earth. Because he knows that he has only a short time to perform his heinous acts, and because of his impending imprisonment for one thousand years (Revelation 20:3), he will unleash all of his brutality and uncleanness upon earth's millions. That is why Revelation 12:12 states, "Woe to the inhabiters of the earth and of the sea! for the devil is come down unto you, having great wrath, because he knoweth that he hath but a short time."

Violence

Remember that Noah's day was also one of violence

(Genesis 6:11). Any person who watches television news today surely realizes that we are going through a period of unprecedented violence and terrorism throughout the world. Information coming to the intelligence community is providing further evidence and new details on the operations of a worldwide international terrorist network, which has been functioning since 1969. They are an organized alliance with roots in Asia, the Middle East, especially Iran, Western Europe, Latin America, and the United States. The network's ideological cement is mixed from Marx and Mao, with proclaimed goals of "world revolution," to be attained through a worldwide war of terror against the advanced states in attempts to undermine their normal way of life and institutions. Libya is considered the armorer of world terrorists, using stock obtained from Moscow. While the scope of the terrorist alliance now is attaining global proportions, the Middle East remains its main base and sanctuary area—backed by Russian arms and manipulation. Today, more than 370 terrorist groups are currently operating in 63 countries—and the casualties have reached an all-time high. A CIA study predicts an increasing number of deaths in the years ahead as terrorists become more sophisticated in their approach. It's reported that terrorists believe that a larger number of casualties may now be necessary to generate the amount of publicity formerly evoked by less bloody operations.

The world is in a precarious position. But we've seen nothing yet. Violence will rear its ugly head in monstrous proportions as terrorists prepare for germ and biological warfare to hold major cities captive. Soon millions will die. When it does occur, could it be the beginning of the Tribulation Hour? But fear not precious flock, Jesus said in Luke

21:9, "When ye shall hear of wars and commotions, be not terrified: for these things must first come" and then adds in verse 31, "When ye do see these things come to pass, know ye that the kingdom [return to earth] of God is nigh at hand [near]."

And many false prophets shall rise, and shall deceive many. And because iniquity shall abound, the love of many shall wax cold. But he that shall endure unto the end, the same shall be saved. And this gospel of the kingdom shall be preached in all the world for a witness unto all nations; and then shall the end come.

Matthew 24:11-14

Question 24

What are the signs of Christ's return?

ow that we have addressed several foundational
questions on the pre-Rapture signs, I want to show
you how the Bible provides overwhelmingly clear
evidence of other pretribulational signs demonstrating
Christ's impending return to earth. I will now begin to deal
with every major sign in the New Testament to show that
Jesus' statement, "When ye shall see all these things, know
that it is near, even at the doors" (Matthew 24:33), is being
fulfilled in our day and age. Matthew 24:3-14 declares:

> And as he [Jesus] sat upon the Mount of Olives, the
> disciples came unto him privately, saying. Tell us,
> when shall these things be? and what shall be the
> sign of thy coming, and of the end of the world?
> And Jesus answered and said unto them, Take heed
> that no man deceive you. For many shall come in my
> name, saying, I am Christ; and shall deceive many.
> And ye shall hear of wars and rumours of wars: see
> that ye be not troubled: for all these things must
> come to pass, but the end is not yet. For nation shall
> rise against nation, and kingdom against kingdom:

and there shall be famines, and pestilences, and earthquakes, in divers places. All these are the beginning of sorrows. Then shall they deliver you up to be afflicted, and shall kill you: and ye shall be hated of all nations for my name's sake. And then shall many be offended, and shall betray one another, and shall hate one another, And many false prophets shall rise, and shall deceive many. And because iniquity shall abound, the love of many shall wax cold. But he that shall endure unto the end, the same shall be saved. And this gospel of the kingdom shall be preached in all the world for a witness unto all nations; and then shall the end come.

This passage may be among the most misunderstood of all prophetic pronouncements. The problem has arisen because many Christians still fail to see that God has two elect groups upon earth—the nation of Israel (Romans 11:28) and the Church (1 Peter 1:2). Romans 9-11 tells the entire story of God's chosen people, Israel. Chapter 9 concerns Israel's past, chapter 10 its present, and chapter 11 its future. Regarding its glorious past, Romans 9:4 declares that Israel was given the promises, including prophetic pledges. In chapter 10, verse 16, we find: "But they have not all obeyed the gospel. For Esaias saith, Lord, who [among them] hath believed our report?" Presently, they are blinded to their calling and promises, but in the future, "All Israel shall be saved: as it is written. There shall come out of Sion the Deliverer, and shall turn away ungodliness from Jacob" (Romans 11:26).

Why will God perform this? Verse 29 provides the answer: "For the gifts and calling of God are without repentance." God chose Israel (Deuteronomy 7:7-8) and He has never canceled His selection. Therefore, Israel remains God's chosen people and heir to His promises as stated in Romans 11:28. The signs of Matthew 24 are presented to the elect— yes, elect Israel. We know this to be true in this chapter because of the regard for the Sabbath day (v. 20), because of the connection with synagogues (Luke 21:12), and because the setting of Matthew 24 is Jerusalem (v. 1). Only Bible manipulators, antidispensationalists, and antiliteralists could make Gentiles out of these Jews.

Included in this group are the twelve tribes of the children of Israel. Twelve thousand shall be chosen from each of the twelve tribes. Twelve thousand times twelve equals 144,000. The tribes are Juda, Reuben, Gad, Aser, Nephthalim, Manasses, Simeon, Levi, Issachar, Zabulon, Joseph, and Benjamin (Revelation 7:4-8). These signs are for Israel, who is looking for the return of her King in Revelation 19. They are not signposts for the Rapture.

The group looking for the fulfillment of signs in Matthew 24 is preaching a different gospel in verse 14. *Gospel* means "good news," and their good news is the gospel of the kingdom or the good news that their King is about to return (Revelation 19:16). They will be traveling around the globe, 144,000 strong, singing "The King is coming! The King is coming!" Although the signs will be fulfilled in their entirety after the Christians are gone, we already see the tantalizing beginning of each of these signs. Again, this means that if these signs pointing to our return with the King are already in their initial stages, we must be snatched away very soon in order to prepare for our return to earth with Christ the King.

The Great Escape

False Christs

In Matthew 24:3, Jesus was asked, "When shall these things be? and what shall be the sign of thy coming [to earth], and of the end of the world [or age of grace]?" He replied, "Many shall come in my name, saying, I am Christ; and shall deceive many" (v. 5). Since the year 1900, more than eleven hundred people claiming to be Christ have appeared on the world scene. These include Father Divine, Prophet Jones, Sweet Daddy Grace, Father Riker; Daniel Swalt, Moses Guibbory, Maharaj Ji, and Sun Myung Moon, not to mention scores of lesser-known, self-proclaimed messiahs who enjoyed a few fleeting moments of media fame.

Presently, while they might not refer to themselves as "false Christs," certain members of our liberal clergy are playing such a role. Take, for example, a survey of the beliefs and attitudes of the Church of Scotland ministers. They have rightfully caused a stir within the denomination as the foun-dational truth of the Bible—the virgin birth of Christ—was recently called into question by religious leaders. The shocking results of the survey of 150 ministers were that 16 percent did not believe in the Immaculate Conception of Christ and 15 percent said that they "didn't know." An amazing 17 percent said that the Virgin Mary was not a virgin in twentieth-century terms, and 6 percent thought that Jesus was the product of Mary and Joseph having sex outside of marriage. (See Matthew 7:21-23 and 2 Peter 2:1-3.)

Such abuse of Scripture is yet another sign of the times. However, eventually, the ultimate false Christ—one who is probably alive even at this moment—will proclaim himself as the true Christ and become accepted on an international scale. The Bible predicts such an hour, when the Antichrist, "who opposeth and exalteth himself above all that is called God, or that is worshipped... sitteth in the temple of God, shewing himself that he is God" (2 Thessalonians 2:4) and is accepted as such. This internationally deified dictator will inaugurate a world-peace program which will hold the world spellbound for forty-two months, or three and one-half years. Then, in the middle of the seven-year period of tribulation, he will break all of his pledges and destroy his contractual obligations with Israel (Daniel 9:27). At this time, Russia will begin a world war as she invades Israel (Ezekiel 38:11). This war will eventually involve all nations (Zechariah 14:2).

This is God's outline from the Bible. First, the international dictator will establish global peace, and when the world believes that Utopia has arrived, the bottom will fall out of their hopes and aspirations: "For when they shall say, Peace and safety; then sudden destruction cometh upon them" (1 Thessalonians 5:3). We now move to even more dramatic signs that signify our Lord is coming soon.

Ye shall hear of wars and rumours of wars: see that ye be not troubled: for all these things must come to pass, but the end is not yet. For nation shall rise against nation, and kingdom against kingdom.

Matthew 24:6-7

Question 25

What is the significance of today's wars, famines, and increasing pestilences?

From the proclamation of Matthew 24:6-7, we see that the world can expect nothing but rivalry and battles until the Antichrist produces the false peace of the Tribulation era. More than 176 limited wars have been fought since the end of the Second World War. Today one out of every four nations on earth is engaged in some kind of military conflict.

Soon, however, we will experience the greatest global confrontation in history, for we are marching swiftly toward Armageddon at this moment. Over a decade ago, CIA and British Intelligence reports about the Soviet Union were grim. They reported the development of new weapons systems located throughout the Soviet Union, along with expenditures of enormous sums for underground civil defense shelters that meant that Russia was preparing for war. Many did not believe these pronouncements at the time.

Even today, while there is a semblance of peace (although the signs of a reemergence of the Cold War are increasing), we must not be lulled into thinking that Russia has changed her ways—especially since enormous numbers of nuclear warheads remain hidden in underground silos throughout the southern provinces of that vast land. I've noted that people no longer laugh at the prophecies uttered by Ezekiel in chapters 38 and 39 that picture the Russian hordes from the north swarming to the Middle East. Today, as the end-time clock continues to wind down, the red horse of the Apocalypse is about to appear. Revelation 6:4 states, "There went out another horse that was red: and power was given to him that sat thereon to take peace from the earth, and that they should kill one another: and there was given unto him a great sword."

Famines and Pestilences

Christ continued in Matthew 24:7, "And there shall be famines, and pestilences." More than two billion of the world's inhabitants go to bed hungry each night. There are nationwide famine in the Sudan and Rwanda and reports of widespread cannibalism in North Korea—with news coming from Indonesia, the earth's fourth largest nation, that millions of people on those scattered islands remain on the brink of starvation. Thousands are dying painful deaths throughout our world, while scores of others are too numb with hunger to realize what is happening. One writer said it poignantly, "First the belly swells, then the hair turns gray and the skin cracks, after a while the victim dies in mute misery." Such an experience will soon be the fate of millions of people. Paul Erlich, a biochemist at Stanford University, said it's already too late to prevent famines that will kill millions, because already one-half billion are starving and another billion are malnourished. He may be right. There seems to be no possible solution in the near future, because it is too late to produce enough food.

America will undoubtedly be included in this suffering in the days ahead. In fact, the number of the beast, 666 (something we'll address in a later question and answer), may come into existence through an international rationing plan. Soon the voice of Revelation 6:6 will sound, "A measure of wheat for a penny." A measure in Bible times was a quart, and a penny was a day's wages. Imagine a loaf of bread for a day's labor. Pestilence, the twin sister of hunger, is also on the rampage. The swine flu scare, legionnaires' disease, AIDS, and other diseases—many already fully resistant to antibiotics and other medications—are only the beginning. Years ago I read an article in *Reader's Digest,* reprinted from an article in *Time* entitled, "The Bugs Are Coming." And they have come indeed . . . and will continue to come in plaguelike fashion during these final days. Even as I write these words, other pestilential plagues are in their preparatory stages. The South American fire ant has advanced from its initial beachhead in Mobile, Alabama, and now infests more than one hundred billion acres in nine southern states, sometimes driving farmworkers from the fields because of its fiery sting. In forest areas the gypsy moth, the spruce budworm, and the southern pine beetle have wreaked devastation on huge areas of woodland, defoliating and killing millions of valuable trees—enough, in fact, to build 910,000 houses per year! Corn borers and rootworms have attacked crops in the Corn Belt at an incredible rate. The boll weevil costs United States farmers millions of dollars in crop losses annually. The mosquito is infecting one million humans per year in Africa and killing thousands annually with malaria, while the black fly in the Volta River basin blinds hundreds of thousands each year.

The Great Escape

The insect world is multiplying at an exponential rate. Entomologists estimate that the number has now climbed to one quintillion, representing five million different species. If a person could weigh all insects together, *their combined weight would be twelve times that of the entire human race.* Can there be any doubt that the pestilence Jesus predicted will soon rear its head in monstrous proportions and that world hunger will be felt by every country on earth? This, along with what comes out of the bottomless pit in Revelation 9:2 (causing the plague of verse 3), is just around the corner. Listen to the prediction: "There came out of the smoke locusts upon the earth: and unto them was given power, as the scorpions of the earth have power." Their purpose is to destroy and kill. The Rapture is near, my friend ... the signs are all around us.

[Jesus also said, There shall be]
earthquakes, in divers places.

Matthew 24:7

And because iniquity shall abound,
the love of many shall wax cold.

Matthew 24:12

For as the lightning cometh out of the east,
and shineth even unto the west; so shall also the
coming of the Son of man be.

Matthew 24:27

Question 26

What about earthquakes, global crime, and the many strange activities presently occurring in space? How do these signs suggest that Christ's return is at hand?

Earthquakes

When they read Matthew 24:7, Mark 13:8, or Luke 21:11, some men foolishly observe, "We've always had earthquakes. How can this be a sign?" The Lord made this prediction around A.D. 30. According to the U.S. Geological Survey, from 1890 to 1930 there were only 8 quakes measuring 6.0 or larger. From 1930 to 1960, there were only 18. From 1960 to 1979, however; there were 64 "killer" quakes. And from 1980 to the present, there have been more than 200. Think of it! More than 200 major quakes in less than three decades—an earth-rattling reminder that the Rapture is near.

Crimes against Humanity

Christ went on to say in His pronouncement of signs, "And because iniquity shall abound, the love of many shall wax cold" (Matthew 24:12). What a portrait of modern-day America and the world! The U.S. Justice Department reports that about 30 percent or more of the nation's households are victimized by serious crime every year. The U.S. attorney general says that on average one of every sixteen American families is brutalized by violent crimes such as murder, rape, and aggravated assault. The FBI index also paints a grim picture, giving us the unsettling information that a murder occurs every twenty-four minutes, a forcible rape each seven minutes, a robbery every sixty-eight seconds, and an aggravated assault each fifty-one seconds. The total figures show that a violent crime is committed every twenty-seven seconds, a property crime every three seconds. Judge for yourself: Are things getting better or worse? The answer is obvious.

Signs in Space

Matthew 24:27-31 tells us: "For as the lightning cometh out of the east, and shineth even unto the west; so shall also the coming of the Son of man be. For wheresoever the carcase is, there will the eagles be gathered together. Immediately after the tribulation of those days shall the sun be darkened, and the moon shall not give her light, and the stars shall fall from heaven, and the powers of the heavens shall be shaken: And then shall appear the sign of the Son of man in heaven: and then shall all the tribes of the earth mourn, and they shall see the Son of man coming in the clouds of heaven with power and great glory. And he shall send his angels with a great sound of a trumpet, and they shall gather together his elect from the four winds, from one end of heaven to the other."

I quote from these scriptures in Matthew because many believers are confused by this scenario. It is important to note that the reference here is to the Revelation—the revealing of Christ to the entire world as He returns to earth as King of kings—not the Rapture. The elect mentioned in this text are the elect Israelites of Romans 11:28. He gathers them together "from the four winds." Gentile believers are not listed with the twelve tribes who mourn as Christ returns. Again, *these are Jewish signs pointing to Christ's coming as King of kings and* LORD *of lords.* The people of the Tribulation Hour will know when the momentous event is near because Matthew 24:29 pinpoints the time: "Immediately after the tribulation of those days shall the sun be darkened, and the moon shall not give her light, and the stars shall fall from heaven, and the powers of the heavens shall be shaken." The space signs are for the close of the Tribulation Hour. There is no way that they could point to the pretribulation Rapture, for we Christians will be gone when the dreadful bombardment of earth, probably with meteorites from space, occurs.

Luke adds to this account, "And there shall be signs in the sun, and in the moon, and in the stars; and upon the earth distress of nations, with perplexity; the sea and the waves roaring; Men's hearts failing them for fear, and for looking after those things which are coming on the earth: for the powers of heaven shall be shaken" (Luke 21:25-26). These signs point to the close of the Tribulation Hour because they signal the return of the King to earth. Verse 27 adds, "Then shall they see the Son of man coming in a cloud with power and great glory." This describes the coming of Christ to set up His glorious millennial reign (Revelation 20:4).

Space signs, which are to take place at the conclusion of the Tribulation Hour or almost seven years after the believers' departure via the Rapture, are already showing partial fulfillment. Such feats as humans walking, driving, and planting a flag on the moon make us realize these signs are only for twentieth-century citizens—for you and me. If a person had made such a prediction at the turn of the century, he would have become a candidate for a mental hospital. Space activity has become so commonplace today that no one even talks about the first step Neil Armstrong took on the moon in 1969.

"We have always had signs," some skeptics say. "Nothing has changed. It's the same as it was in Grandma's day." My response to that ostrich stance is simply to *get your head out of the sand and fix your eyes on the heavens.* The Space Age is with us, and Christ's prophecies are occurring with such rapidity that only a hardened heart could doubt it. Eventually, scientists and engineers will shoot solar cells across miles of space to beam electricity to earth via microwaves. Each new venture will incorporate additional methods of placing the potentials of space on earth. Christ's astounding prophetic statements about space are beginning to fill the skies. Some scientists and space writers are raising the possibility that the next large-scale war could be fought entirely in space. This possibility means that Satan and his demonic hosts could use the world's inventions for the war of wars described in Revelation 12:7-9: "And there was war in heaven: Michael and his angels fought against the dragon; and the dragon fought and his angels, And prevailed not; neither was their place found any more in heaven. And the great dragon was cast out, that old serpent, called the Devil, and Satan, which deceiveth the whole world: he was cast out into the earth, and his angels were cast out with him."

Question 26

The Signs and Space Phenomena

I believe the rash of reports about UFOs are connected with the spirit world. The question "Is there life on other planets?" is unimportant. There is life in the heavens, for they are full of live, demonic spirits. This could easily explain the thousands of saucer sightings in recent years. Ezekiel 1 and 2 Kings 2:11 talk about angels and chariots of fire. Whoever controls them is incidental. What *is* important is that these strange signs in space are prophesied for the latter days. Those days are now upon us and should make us realize the coming of the Savior is near.

I know thy works, that thou art neither cold nor hot:
I would thou wert cold or hot.
So then because thou art lukewarm, and neither cold
nor hot, I will spue thee out of my mouth.

Revelation 3:15-16

Question 27

Do Old Testament signs primarily speak of Christ's return to earth? What about the signs in the Epistles?

I am asked this question repeatedly. While the Old Testament and four Gospels are filled with scores of references to Christ's return or the Revelation, the Epistles also contain a rich storehouse of scripture that speaks about Christ's return to earth. Look at the description in 2 Timothy 3:1-5: "This know also, that in the last days perilous times shall come. For men shall be lovers of their own selves, covetous, boasters, proud, blasphemers, disobedient to parents, unthankful, unholy. Without natural affection, trucebreakers, false accusers, incontinent, fierce, despisers of those that are good. Traitors, heady, highminded, lovers of pleasure more than lovers of God; Having a form of godliness, but denying the power thereof: from such turn away."

Let's look at several of the signs—as recorded in the Epistles—concerning the return of our Lord and Savior Jesus Christ to earth.

Selfishness

"Men shall be lovers of their own selves." What a picture of the hour in which we live. You do not need to watch CNN for more than a few minutes to understand that people are living a life dedicated to self. Moreover, it is not only unbelievers who live such lives. When church members are so busy satisfying their flesh with the world's goodies and pleasures that they have no time to pray or witness to lost souls—that is the height of selfishness. You will remember the Bible passage about the scribe who came to Jesus in Matthew 22:36-40 and said, "Master, which is the great commandment... ? Jesus said unto him. Thou shalt love the Lord thy God with all thy heart, and with all thy soul, and with all thy mind. This is the first and great commandment. And the second is like unto it. Thou shalt love thy neighbour as thyself. On these two commandments hang all the law and the prophets."

How different are we today, really? We, too, are lovers of our own selves. A person might expect this attitude in the ungodly world of pagans, but how sad when it occurs among those who are supposedly of the family of God. As selfishness accelerates and becomes the central theme at the beginning of a new century, you can be sure it is a sign that the end of the age is near.

The Love of Money

In the first century, Peter could say, "Silver and gold have I none; but such as I have give I thee; In the name of Jesus Christ of Nazareth rise up and walk" (Acts 3:6). Churches today have incredible wealth. We build huge buildings and enjoy elaborate campuses. Much of this is good. However it is also a problem for many ministries, because the tail is wagging the dog. Furthermore, money does not have the power to perform miracles. As we approach the return of Christ, we need to recognize that we are living in the Laodicean age. Revelation 3:15-16 declares, "I know thy works, that thou art neither cold nor hot: I would thou wert cold or hot. So then because thou art lukewarm, and neither cold nor hot, I will spue thee out of my mouth." God is saying, "You lukewarm parishioners make Me sick!" Why? "Because thou sayest, I am rich, and increased with goods, and have need of nothing: and knowest not that thou art wretched, and miserable, and poor, and blind, and naked" (v. 17). Our world is getting poorer and poorer.

In our churches, many regard themselves as "upper crust." They have money, power, and influence. Many of these Christian elite personalities feel they are too important to help others or to carry out acts of kindness in the Savior's name—no time for anything except to earn a few more dollars. God declares, "The love of money is the root of all evil: which while some coveted after, they have erred from the faith, and pierced themselves through with many sorrows" (1 Timothy 6:10).

Pride

God says, "Humble yourselves in the sight of the Lord, and he shall lift you up" (James 4:10). Satan fell because of pride. Moreover millions more have followed in his wake. Imagine the gall Satan must have had to say, "I will ascend into heaven, I will exalt my throne above the stars of God: I will sit also upon the mount of the congregation, in the sides of the north: I will ascend above the heights of the clouds; I will be like the most High" (Isaiah 14:13-14).

Satan has infiltrated the hearts of millions of Christians.

The Great Escape

A man with tears in his eyes once came to me and said, "I was trying to win a young lady to Christ. She was poor and needy. Her parents are alcoholics. She was so destitute that all she had to wear was an old tattered dress. I took her to our church—a Bible-believing fellowship. When she and I walked down the aisle to our seats, I overheard a few snooty people behind me say, "Why do they bring that kind of trash to *our* church!'" That kind of story breaks my heart, and I hope it breaks yours. However, if you feel your pedigree is better or more important than others, then I pray that God will speak to you and show you that *you are one of the signs that Jesus Christ is coming again.* Our Savior said, "Come unto me, all ye that labour and are heavy laden, and I will give you rest. Take my yoke upon you, and learn of me; for I am meek and lowly in heart: and ye shall find rest unto your souls" (Matthew 11:28-29).

Children, obey your parents in the Lord: for this is right.
Honour thy father and mother; which is the
first commandment with promise . . .
and thou mayest live long on the earth.

Ephesians 6:1-3

Question 28

Why are behavioral attitudes such as blasphemy,
disobedience, lack of gratitude, ungodliness,
lying, and broken promises
signs of Christ's return?

Sinful attitudes which move us away from a holy God
have been with us since the fall of man. If you read
world history, however, you will notice the sins of humankind have become progressively worse—some would
say *more creative in their evil.* The bad news is that tomorrow they even become worse (2 Timothy 3:13). Let us look
at the six signs of Christ's imminent return referred to in
the above question.

Blasphemy

Blasphemy is a sin against the Lord Jesus Christ. The
apostle Paul indicated that he "was before a blasphemer" (1
Timothy 1:13). What had Paul done? He murdered Christians
and hated the name of Jesus Christ. Today the physical murder of Christians continues unabated. I recently received
two reports of hundreds of Christians who are being persecuted for their faith in the nations of China and India. The
name of Jesus is not honored in those places. Pastors are
being thrown in jail; individual Christians must worship in
secret, lest they be taken before the authorities. In many

places of our world, the name of Jesus is blasphemed, and Christians are suspect. In fact, this would be a good time to pray for Christians throughout the world who serve the Master faithfully in difficult places, even as it puts them in danger.

However, let us keep the issue on our own doorsteps for a moment. Many so-called Christians are equally blasphemous. Scores of our seminaries, for example, are filled with students and professors who mock the doctrine of the Lord Jesus Christ, His virgin birth, His deity, blood atonement, and bodily resurrection. Intelligent scholars teach a "higher criticism" of the Bible when, in fact, they proclaim the *lowest form* of interpretation possible because, in their disbelief, they blaspheme the Christ of the Scriptures. Surveys indicate that 70 percent of our ministers are infected by this spiritual sickness. God help us if these statistics are accurate. Can there be any doubt that Jesus Christ is coming soon?

Disobedience

There is nothing new about this sin, particularly when it comes to children disobeying their parents. Some young people say that they love Jesus Christ, yet when their parents make requests, they treat them disrespectfully and are willfully disobedient. Do these alleged Christian youth really believe the message of God's Word? It makes me wonder. Ephesians 6:1-3 admonishes, "Children, obey your parents in the Lord: for this is right. Honour thy father and mother; which is the first commandment with promise ... and thou mayest live long on the earth."

Question 28

I was moved recently as I studied John 19:26-27. These verses portray Jesus Christ hanging on the cross, dying for our sins. As He was about to die, He looked down and saw His mother, Mary, standing beneath the cross. "Woman, behold thy son! Then saith he to the disciple, Behold thy mother!" Even in the last moments of life, as He was dying for the entire world, the Lord Jesus Christ fervently loved His mother. He came to fulfill the law, and He said in Matthew 19:19, "Honour thy father and thy mother." The growing numbers of disobedient and disrespectful young people are a sign that Jesus is coming soon. We must remember that freedom is not license to do anything we want; freedom is the privilege God gives us to *do the right thing!* Disobedience to human authority and to God is on the rise; it is one of the major signs that signal Christ's return.

Ingratitude

Many people—Christians included—find it difficult to give credit where credit is due. Because they seek their own glory, they refuse to recognize the accomplishments and contributions of others whom God has sent to share the labor and service. Many simply do not take the time to say, "Thank You, Lord" for answered prayer. Still others are ashamed to pray in a restaurant. When they do bow their heads, they sit there and scratch their eyebrows for a few seconds so no one will think they are talking to Almighty God. My friend, of what are we afraid? Has the world so squeezed us into its own mold that we are indistinguishable from the world system? Are you thankful? Do you have an attitude of gratitude? Show it!

Unholy

What a graphic picture of our world as we step into a new millennium. During the end times, godly separation from the world, according to the Bible, will be sneered at as bigotry. When one rails against XXX-rated movies, the lewd lyrics of much of today's rock music, the cancer-producing effects of tobacco (including smokeless tobacco), the soul-damning habits of drugs and alcohol, some Christians immediately change the subject and say, "Let's not talk about secondary issues."

The holiness of God and holy living are not secondary issues. First Thessalonians 4:7 declares, "For God hath not called us unto uncleanness, but unto holiness." First Peter 1:16 teaches, "Be ye holy; for I am holy." Again, this sign indicates that Jesus is coming soon. I encourage you to read God's Word and come to your own conclusions. All the signs in 2 Timothy 3 speak of Christendom and the professing Church in the last days. These final days are now upon us.

Lack of Love and Broken Promises

The phrase, "Without natural affection" (2 Timothy 3:3), refers to the breakup of families through a lack of love. Look at the divorce rate, the murder of babies through abortion, the stories about parents beating their little ones to death, and you will know this sign is being fulfilled. For millions, the marriage vow has become a cruel joke. For millions, *commitment* is a word in a foreign tongue. Broken promises are the order of the day. Has someone shared a confidence entreating your prayer support? Did you keep it, or did you spread gossip about that person? Promise breaking is a pivotal *end-time sign* mentioned in the Bible. While stadiums around the world are filled with promise *keepers,* unfortunately there are more living rooms, board-rooms, and bedrooms filled with promise *breakers.*

Lying

"False accusers" (v. 3) is the term that refers to this sin. Churches in our nation and around the globe are coming apart at the seams because of exaggerated stories (outright lies in many cases) church members spread about their so-called friends. When a person falsely accuses a brother, he breaks God's ninth commandment. Exodus 20:16 says, "Thou shalt not bear false witness." Do you know what will happen to false accusers? Revelation 21:8 says, "But the fearful, and unbelieving, and the abominable, and murderers, and whoremongers, and sorcerers, and idolaters, and all liars, shall have their part in the lake which burneth with fire and brimstone." You will notice that in this book, I am coming down harder on Christians than on unbelievers. We who say we honor Christ should know better. We are held to a higher standard than those who do not know the Savior, Yes, the end-time clock is ticking faster and faster; sins of the flesh and the spirit will increase; lying and half-truths will continue unabated. That is why during these perilous times you and I must remain firm, believe what we say we believe, and stand in the gap as we anticipate the return of our Lord in all His glory.

Let all bitterness, and wrath, and anger, and clamour,
and evil speaking, be put away from you,
with all malice: And be ye kind one to another,
tenderhearted, forgiving one another,
even as God for Christ's sake hath forgiven you.

Ephesians 4:31-32

Question 29

*What about a world that is out of control,
with an increasing number of murders and
sex-on-demand overtures on the Internet?
Are these signs that the return of
our Lord is near?*

We live in a world that is spinning out of control. Murder is on the increase. Students in our high schools are killing their classmates and their parents. Virtual-reality sex on the Internet is becoming a national pastime for adults and children alike. Our loved ones are increasingly at risk as they download material of prurient interest now available at the click of a mouse button in the privacy of one's own home. Still, for all the "power" supposedly available to our citizens, people are more powerless than ever. *What does the Bible say about such pursuits? How do such sins suggest that the return of Christ may be near?*

In Matthew 7:18 we read that a good tree cannot bear bad fruit, nor can a bad tree bear good fruit. This is what we are seeing in our society today. There are lots of "trees" growing all around us. The good ones honor God and bring glory to His name. The bad ones, however, continue to put forth branches that are diseased and deformed. Let us look at the four areas mentioned in this question.

The Great Escape

No Self-Control

Incontinent would be the best term to define this problem. It speaks of the lack of control over one's sexual appetites. The world says, "Live it up. Premarital and extramarital sex are good and healthy—just be 'safe' with your sex." I say, "Let God be true, but every man a liar" (Romans 3:4). Sex is pure and holy in marriage. Hebrews 13:4 states, "Marriage is honourable in all, and the bed undefiled." However; the verse continues, "whoremongers and adulterers God will judge." What God demands and what our society craves are light-years apart. Look at these four statistics:

1. One out of every two marriages ends in divorce.

2. The average age today for divorce is thirty-four for men and thirty for women.

3. In the 1960s, a woman was responsible for one of every ten households with no husband present; in 1986, a woman carried out her duties in one of every six households with no husband present.

4. One million teenage girls will become pregnant out of wedlock this year.

Temper

Some men would be minus their front teeth if they spoke to the server in a restaurant like they talk to their wives at home. They claim they love Jesus Christ. They are great Christians at church, but what a fierce, vicious temper they exhibit at home and at work. Anger is killing people on the freeways; it is responsible for accelerated spousal and child abuse, and it is destroying relationships at the office and in the church. The Bible says, "Let all bitterness, and wrath, and anger, and clamour, and evil speaking, be put away from you, with all malice" (Ephesians 4:31). My friend, when a person has not been redeemed by the love of Christ, he or she will fall prey to an angry spirit. When this unholy spirit takes over a family, a community, a state, a nation, and a world, we know that the end is near.

Pleasure

"Lovers of pleasures more than lovers of God" (2 Timothy 3:4). In the last days, people—professing Christians included—will be lovers of pleasure more than lovers of our heavenly Father. We have become a nation—and a world— of hedonists. This sign is evident as churches increasingly use the tactics of the entertainment business to draw crowds. People want to be amused; so many churches feel they must meet the cravings of their pleasure-mad constituents. How else are the lukewarm and backslidden going to be held together? How else can halfhearted members be attracted to the services? Consequently, the latest Christian minstrel show takes the place of the Word of God.

God has not called us to run a showboat to entertain those who would be amused but a lifeboat to save the lost from ultimate destruction. Many religious telecasts and crusades today feature unsaved or carnal personalities whose lives are a mockery to God. Still, they appear because entertainers draw crowds. Many evangelistic meetings feature folks who are still working in nightclubs where drinking, gambling, filthy jokes, and solicitation of sex are prevalent. Is this a sign of the end or what! The organizers rationalize their activity by saying, "It does not matter, because the end justifies the means. If these religious fakes draw crowds, then it must be the right thing to do." God forgive us!

Through it all, people without Christ are lulled to sleep and made to feel religious while every carnal desire of the flesh is gratified under the sanction of the Church. Will this continue? Yes, I am afraid it will. That is why it behooves Bible-believing Christians to stand up and be counted on this issue.

Lack of Power

We eat power lunches, wear power ties, demand more horsepower in our automobiles, and ingest power vitamins. Power, power, power. The Bible talks a great deal about our quest for this power, which is, in reality, a false sense of security. Paul wrote to Timothy, "Having a form of godliness, but denying the power thereof (2 Timothy 3:5). It should be obvious by now that the world system has no staying power. Zero! What concerns me more is that there is so little power in the Church. How could it be otherwise, when the Church has strayed so far from seeking and doing God's will? Study this sign in the Scriptures, and you will be compelled to come to one conclusion: Soon the trumpet of God shall sound and we shall hear three words, "Come up hither" (Revelation 4:1). Then, in the twinkling of an eye, we will sweep through the heavens to meet Jesus.

There are seven kings: five are fallen, and one is, and the other is not yet come; and when he cometh, he must continue a short space.

Revelation 17:10

Question 30

I have heard a great deal about the European "Superstate" and the coming "New World Order." Are these events also signs of Christ's return?

The short answer is Yes! We are living at a time in which it is not only possible for a world dictator of unprecedented authority to emerge—the Antichrist— it is also inevitable. God's Word states that only seven empires will exist in world history before Christ returns. The verse proving this statement is Revelation 17:10, "There are seven kings: five are fallen, and one is, and the other is not yet come; and when he cometh, he must continue a short space." The five fallen empires referred to by John in this verse are Assyria, Egypt, Babylon, Medo-Persia, and Greece. The one that ruled at the time John wrote the Book of Revelation was Rome. One more final empire would arise, but there would first be a long delay. That global power would be the "revived Roman Empire," a scenario we addressed briefly in an earlier question. From this final group of nations the figure known as the Antichrist emerges and reigns for a brief period—just eighty-four months. So the question: Is this period way off in the distant future? No! *It is around the corner.* The world is on the brink of submission to this latter-day power. This revived Roman Empire is presently assembling and organizing itself under the aegis of the European Union, a federal Superstate that will form the basis for the last one-world government. This dictatorship under Antichrist rules with supernatural power, advanced twenty-first-century technological police-state know-how, and unthinkable terror. Is it in the making? Judge for yourself. The European Community created the European Monetary Institute in January 1994, and it is scheduled to become a central bank issuing a single currency no later than 2002.

In addition to its growing economic prowess, the European Union will formulate common foreign and security policies with defense issues handled by the Western European Union. Soon, all defense policies will be made jointly. The European Union is rapidly dissolving the ideas of national sovereignty in a giant step toward globalism and one-world government. The Superstate is preparing the way for a more powerful central government, one that will eventually be headed by a world dictator. In Daniel 9:27, we see this future Führer making a peace contract with the nations of the earth for seven years. During the first half of this tribulational period, the Antichrist is controlled by satanic powers (Revelation 13:4). However, during the second forty-two months, Satan is cast out of heaven (Revelation 12:7-11) and incarnates the body of this world dictator (Revelation 13:3). When Satan takes over the physical being of the Antichrist, he begins to call himself god, magnifying himself above every god (Daniel 11:36).

How can we know with certainty that we are close to this historical moment? The entire prophetic scenario began in the miraculous year of 1948, when three major world events occurred simultaneously. The first was the rebirth of the land of Israel. Jesus Himself predicted this event would precede His return in Matthew 24:32-33 when He told His disciples to come to grips with the message of the parable of the fig tree, which always represents Israel in the Bible. Jesus said, "When his branch is yet tender, and putteth forth leaves, ye know that summer is nigh: So likewise ye, when ye shall see all these things, know that it is near, even at the doors." Nothing of significance prophetically, therefore, could happen until Israel became a nation again. That happened in 1948. In addition, that year witnessed the first meeting that would lead to the establishment of the revived Roman Empire, the European Union. This last-days entity would form the political and military basis for the coming one-world government—the apparatus by which the Antichrist would rule. The third important event of 1948 was the formation of the World Council of Churches, which would help lay the groundwork for the one-world religious system of the Antichrist described in Revelation 13:11 and 17:9. For more than fifty years now, the stage has been set for a world dictator to emerge, a man with power and authority far beyond the scope of Nebuchadnezzar or any of his successors. The world anxiously awaits his appearance. I have little doubt that this great imposter is alive and waiting in the wings. How close are we to the fateful day of his appearance? Here is what three citizens say:

"We are in a leaderless world," is the opinion of Walter Cronkite.

"We have a rendezvous with a world dictator and his appearance may be soon," says economist Julian Snyder.

The internationally acclaimed Dr. Paul-Henri Spaak says, "Europe is looking for a man so powerful that he will hold the allegiance of all the people. Be he man or devil we are ready to receive him."

However, it is not just a political leader for whom the world is looking. All the major religions discuss the emergence, in the last days, of a powerful and terrifying spiritual figure—someone who will ultimately proclaim himself to be God. Today's widespread New Age philosophy is laying the groundwork for the Antichrist's global religious system. Did you know, for instance, that John Randolph Price, one of the world's principal New Age gurus, says his spirit guide revealed to him that 2.5 billion people may need to be wiped off the face of the earth for their Utopian spiritual dreams to be realized (Revelation 6:8; 9:18; 13:15; 20:4)? Could such an organization claiming a billion followers produce the Antichrist? Definitely!

The New Age movement teaches that we are all "little gods." I believe the Antichrist will ride the crest of that belief and give it the credibility it does not deserve. However, the honeymoon for the Antichrist will not last forever. He will suffer a mortal head wound and come to his end in a battle with Russia (Daniel 11:45). After being incarnated by Satan, he then rises from the dead and declares himself as the god of gods (Revelation 13:3). He demands that every human being worship him under penalty of death (Revelation 13:15). Is it not fitting that today's New Age leaders are already beginning to justify the mass slaughter that will follow? The Antichrist will have more help, too, from someone known as "the false prophet." It is from the leadership of this false prophet, propped up by the revived European Empire, that all such latter-day prophecies emerge. Rome will again be the center of the world economically, politically, militarily, and spiritually. Those currently moving Europe in this direction seem inexplicably drawn to their fate. Perhaps you remember that in 1987, the Belgians minted the first ECU silver coins. Imprinted on them was the bust of Emperor Charles the Fifth, crowned head of the Holy Roman Empire in 1519. Why was Charles chosen to be immortalized on the first-ever European coin? Because of the striking geographical similarity between the European Community and the Holy Roman Empire. But what about the ten toes and the ten nations? Hasn't the European Union evolved past this stage? Yes it has. That is to be expected. Remember that we are speaking of an eventual world government, not a regional one. The European Union began as ten nations. In fact, Daniel 7:24 shows us that a very significant eleventh nation arises.

That was Spain. Now we have fifteen and Poland and others may come aboard by the year 2002 for the formation of the one-world government or New World Order. The European Superstate, I believe, will provide the platform and the structure for this world dictatorship (Daniel 7:23; Revelation 13:7). When Christ returns to establish His earthly kingdom, a grouping of ten kings or ten areas remain (Daniel 2:44). Interestingly, all of the prime movers behind the globalist dream have divided the world into ten spheres. The Trilateral Commission, the Council on Foreign Relations, the Bilderbergers, the Club of Rome, and others that promote a one-world federation eventually break up the globe into ten regions. *One way or another God's Word will come to pass.* Only now, after two great European wars have been fought and reunification has occurred, could the promises of the Bible about a world government centered in Rome be possible. Likewise, only now, as we prepare to enter the twenty-first-century computer age could such a government hope to keep track of the commercial activities of every human being on the planet (Revelation 13:16-17). The University of Edinburgh once was proud to claim it had a computer that was able to perform forty billion arithmetic transactions per second. However, that is only one of the ten fastest computers in the world! We now have computers that process upwards of one trillion pieces of information per second. What an up-to-date book is the Bible!

Soon the Rapture will occur, after which a time of unmitigated terror will engulf the globe. "Alas! for that day is great, so that none is like it" (Jeremiah 30:7). Daniel 12:1 describes it as a "time of trouble, such as never was since there was a nation." Jesus used almost the exact words in Matthew 24:21, "For then shall be great tribulation, such as was not since the beginning of the world." These things must happen. They are right around the corner. But we should have no fear about them, not as believers, anyway. When these things come to pass, be not terrified (see Luke 21:9). Why? Because Jesus said that when these things come to pass, "Know ye that the kingdom of God is nigh at hand" (Luke 21:31). We believers who are prepared will miss this horrendous hour. We will be gone before any part of the seven-year Tribulation period begins. We will be caught up in the air to meet Jesus in the twinkling of an eye, according to 1 Corinthians 15:51-54. Then we shall return with the King seven years later to rule and reign (Revelation 20:4). Soon we will hear the shout "Come up hither"! (Revelation 4:1). Then eighty-four months later, the Lord returns with His heavenly entourage for the millennial honeymoon (Jude 14; Revelation 19:7-8, 14; 20:4). My friend, the Rapture is near!

Who opposeth and exalteth himself above all that is called God, or that is worshipped; so that he as God sitteth in the temple of God, shewing himself that he is God.

2 Thessalonians 2:4

Question 31

Who is the coming "worldruler"? What is his
role in end-time prophecy? Will his appearance
have any connection with the rebuilding of the
Temple in Jerusalem?

In Revelation 13:1 the apostle John states, "And I stood
upon the sand of the sea, and saw a beast rise up out
of the sea, having seven heads and ten horns, and upon
his horns ten crowns, and upon his heads the name of blasphemy." The ten horns of John's vision correspond to the
ten toes of Daniel's image in chapter 2 of the Book of Daniel.
Let's investigate this account and see its importance in our
discussion concerning the "coming world ruler." Nebuchadnezzar, the king of ancient Babylon, had a dream. However,
he could not recall its content. Therefore, he called in his
magicians, astrologers, and soothsayers, saying, not very
politely, I might add, "Tell me what I dreamed, or I'll kill
you." That certainly got their attention. However, they
were stymied: They could not fulfill this bizarre request.
However, Daniel, a young Jew and a man of prayer, fell on
his knees three times a day before his God Jehovah and
received the answer.

> The secret which the king hath demanded cannot
> the wise men, the astrologers, the magicians, the
> soothsayers, shew unto the king; But there is a God
> in heaven that revealeth secrets, and maketh known

to the king Nebuchadnezzar what shall be in the latter days. Thy dream, and the visions of thy head upon thy bed, are these . . . Thou, O king, sawest, and behold a great image. This great image, whose brightness was excellent, stood before thee; and the form thereof was terrible. This image's head was of fine gold, his breast and his arms of silver, his belly and his thighs of brass. His legs of iron, his feet part of iron and part of clay. Thou sawest till that a stone was cut out without hands, which smote the image upon his feet that were of iron and clay, and brake them to pieces. Then was the iron, the clay, the brass, the silver, and the gold, broken to pieces together, and became like the chaff of the summer threshingfloors; and the wind carried them away, that no place was found for them: and the stone that smote the image became a great mountain, and filled the whole earth. . . . Thou, O king, art a king of kings: for the God of heaven hath given thee a kingdom, power, and strength, and glory. . . . Thou art this head of gold. And after thee shall arise another kingdom inferior to thee, and another third kingdom of brass, which shall bear rule over all the earth. And the fourth kingdom shall be strong as iron: forasmuch as iron breaketh in pieces and subdueth all things: and as iron that breaketh all these, shall it break in pieces and bruise. And whereas thou sawest the feet and toes, part of potters' clay, and part of iron, the kingdom shall be divided; but there shall be in it of the strength of the iron, forasmuch as thou sawest the iron mixed with miry clay. (Daniel 2:27-28, 31-35, 37-41)

Question 31

Those who scoff, ridicule, and slander the Word of God would be well advised to dust off their history books to discover the reliability of the Bible. In this passage we see that Daniel gave King Nebuchadnezzar an outline of world history down to the last days—events that have taken place precisely as God said they would. Daniel said, "You, King Nebuchadnezzar, are the head of gold (Babylon), but there will be two nations pictured by the arms of silver (the Medes and the Persians) who will destroy you. Then there will be a kingdom of brass (Greece), pictured by the stomach, which will destroy the Medes and the Persians. Next, the kingdom of iron (Rome), pictured by two legs, will smash Greece." Why two legs? Because at one time in history, the Roman Empire was divided, having headquarters both at Rome and Constantinople. Again, a historical fact.

Notice carefully that the only power not put out of existence is the Roman Empire. At the end time, the iron again manifests itself in the toes of the image. It is a deteriorated form mingled with clay, but still viable.

Edward Gibbon's masterpiece *The History of the Decline and Fall of the Roman Empire* reminds us that Rome was never destroyed but rather lost its prominence because of degradation and sin. This historical fact fits the *clay of deterioration.* Nonetheless, the Roman Empire will be revived in the last days through an alignment of ten Western nations, pictured by the ten toes of Daniel's image and the ten horns in the Book of Revelation. In verse 44 of chapter 2, Daniel says, "And in the days of these kings [the confederacy of ten Western nations] shall the God of heaven set up a kingdom, which shall never be destroyed; and the kingdom shall not be left to other people, but it shall break in pieces and consume all these kingdoms, and it shall stand for ever." This refers to the return of Messiah, the

Lord Jesus Christ, which we know is very near.

Consider Daniel 2:34 again: "Thou sawest till that a stone was cut out without hands, which smote the image upon his feet that were of iron and clay, and brake them to pieces." What, or better who, is the stone that smashes the image when the ten Western nations have aligned themselves? Acts 4:11: "[Christ] is the stone which was set at nought of you builders." First Corinthians 10:4: "And that Rock [or stone] was Christ." Since 1948, we have witnessed an amalgamation of Western nations in the form of the European Economic Community or "Common Market." The movement began with Belgium, Luxembourg, and the Netherlands joining in economic alliance. Then France, Italy, and West Germany joined in 1957. In 1972, three additional members—Denmark, England, and Ireland—were received. Then, on January 1, 1981, Greece became the ratified tenth member. However, Ireland and Denmark were never part of the old Roman Empire. What about them? The answer is simple. Daniel 7:8 states, "I considered the horns [at the end time], and, behold, there came up among them [the ten] another little horn [number 11!], before whom there were three of the first horns plucked up by the roots." Once a ten-nation Western confederacy has been formed, number eleven comes to power, plucks up three of the first ten, and replaces them with his own and two others. Later the majority of the globe is under his control. This leader will be the world dictator and infamous Antichrist—the final global ruler.

The organization of the European Economic Community is important because the first beast, or Antichrist of the Book of Revelation, comes out of such an alignment of Western nations. In Revelation 13:1, John says, "I stood upon the sand of the sea, and saw a beast rise up out of the sea." The sea speaks of nations, and the ten toes of Daniel's image and the ten horns of Revelation 13:1 describe a grouping of ten nations. Because this prophecy is now in the early stages of fulfillment, the stage is being set for a powerful world leader who works through this grouping of Western nations until he is able to assume worldwide prominence for his "greatness." We know that he will come from the West because Daniel 9:26 states that he is of the people that destroyed the city and the sanctuary. Who are these people?

As we have already seen, in A.D. 70, Titus, the Roman general from the Western nations of the old Roman Empire, entered Jerusalem, destroyed the Temple, and drove a million of God's people, the Jews, to every part of the earth. Now the prophet says that it is of this people that the Antichrist shall come. With this information in hand, it becomes clear this ruler will arise from the coming together of these Western nations. This appearance of the Antichrist then leads to another important question: the rebuilding of the Temple in Jerusalem—another major sign of Christ's return.

The Rebuilding of the Temple

The Antichrist will come into prominence and power by signing a seven-year peace contract with Israel (Daniel 9:27). Three and a half years after its signing, he will proclaim himself to be God, the true Messiah, and will set himself up as the global ruler in a temple in Jerusalem. Study carefully 2 Thessalonians 2:4, "Who opposeth and exalteth himself above all that is called God, or that is worshipped; so that he as God sitteth in the temple of God, shewing himself that he is God." During our visit to the

Holy Land, I stood by the Wailing Wall in Jerusalem, walked through an arch at the end of the wall, and looked into a great hole in the earth. I observed that there the Jews are attempting to find, as they approach areas of the Dome of the Rock, the Holy of Holies of the old Temple. (Some have indicated through news reports that the Holy of Holies has already been discovered.) They know that the Wailing Wall is part of the old Temple area, and they say, "As soon as we find the Holy of Holies, we will try to build." Chills ran down my spine when I heard them say this, because they were speaking ancient words of prophecy in the twentieth century!

An organization called "The Association for Progress in the Rebuilding of the Holy Temple" has four objectives: (1) to rebuild the Temple in Jerusalem, (2) to enlist scholars to research laws and traditions relating to Temple worship, (3) to set up a fund to receive contributions from Jews in all nations for rebuilding, and (4) to enlist architects, builders, and designers to draw up the plans. What is preventing them from accomplishing their task? According to the Jewish press, the status of the organization is holding back its work because the Israeli government does not want to incite further Arab hatred. Meanwhile, Israel continues to prepare for the rebuilding of the Temple in her own way. Excavations around the Wailing Wall have outlined the boundaries of the old Temple site.

An exciting parallel to the rebuilding of the Temple concerns the $14 million Jerusalem Great Synagogue, which was dedicated August 4, 1982. Built adjoining the "Hechal Schlomo" near the intersection of King George V and Ramban Streets in the new part of Jerusalem, the edifice is only about a mile west of the old Temple site. The synagogue is intended as a rallying point for world Jewry and as a house of prayer. (The Lord Jesus referred to the old Temple as "the house of prayer" in Matthew 21:13.) Interestingly, construction of the Jerusalem Great Synagogue took seven years, plus eleven months of delays, to complete. Students of the Bible will recall that King Solomon's original Temple also took seven years to construct—with an additional eleven-month delay! In addition, consider the facts that (1) a symbolic "half shekel" offering was received from Jews around the world to finance construction costs; (2) the number of $50,000 donors was limited to twelve as was the number of $25,000 donors. These figures equal the number of the tribes of Israel and, combined, equal the twenty-four elders seated around Christ's throne in Revelation 4:4; (3) the synagogue presidents are limited to seventy, the number of elders who once comprised the Sanhedrin. Although the Jews prefer to call this building a *synagogue* rather than a *temple,* one of the chief rabbis insists, "We must never believe that this is a substitute for the temple"—observers note that the Great Synagogue could serve well as the Tribulation Temple. The building contains a symbolic Ark of the Covenant (which the actual ark could replace if or when it is discovered in the old Temple excavation) and a bema seat. The Temple is constructed of the same Jerusalem limestone as Solomon's Temple. Although there is no sacrificial altar at present, one could easily be constructed and made ready to use. Continue to read your papers and watch the day-by-day unfolding of this greatest prophecy of all—the rebuilding of the Temple in Jerusalem—a major sign pointing to the return of the King of kings and Lord of lords who sits in His holy temple upon His arrival to earth in Ezekiel chapters 40-48.

And the beast which I saw was like unto a leopard, and his feet were as the feet of a bear, and his mouth as the mouth of a lion: and the dragon gave him his power, and his seat, and great authority. And I saw one of his heads as it were wounded to death; and his deadly wound was healed: and all the world wondered after the beast.

Revelation 13:2-3

Question 32

Who will be called the "dragon"? Why will the
"dragon" be so powerful in the last days?
What part will he play in the revived
Roman Empire?

To answer this question I would like to present two more of the greatest signs mentioned in the Bible. In Revelation 13:1-2, John says, "And I stood upon the sand of the sea, and saw a beast rise up out of the sea, having seven heads and ten horns, and upon his horns ten crowns, and upon his heads the name of blasphemy.... The dragon gave him his power, and his seat, and great authority." This prophecy predicts a period of global government under a world leader. His power will be given to him by Satan, called "the dragon" (Revelation 13:2).

I would encourage you to refer to two Bibles. In one, turn to Revelation 13; in the other, find Daniel chapters 2 and 7. You will discover, perhaps to your amazement, that these two portions of Scripture, written hundreds of years apart, present identical historical facts. Let us review this material.

Nebuchadnezzar, great king of ancient Babylon, one night had a dream, but forgot its content. He immediately requested that his magicians and soothsayers identify the dream and its interpretation. None of his enchanters were able to meet his demands. Only Daniel, God's man, was able to fulfill the king's request. The report is recorded in Daniel 2:31-36. Verses 31-33 state, "Thou, O king, sawest, and behold a great image. This great image, whose brightness was excellent, stood before thee; and the form thereof was terrible. This image's head was of fine gold, his breast and his arms of silver, his belly and his thighs of brass. His legs of iron, his feet part of iron and part of clay."

The interpretation is located in verses 37—43. Here is a synopsis of the text. Daniel said: Nebuchadnezzar, you are the head of gold. However, your glory will soon be diminished— that is because the two arms of silver, representing the nations of Media and Persia, shall flatten your empire. Furthermore, as history continues, the Medes and Persians will suffer defeat at the hands of the Greeks, typified by the stomach of brass. Then, as the years pass, the iron legs of the Roman Empire shall dethrone Greece from its pedestal of power.

Every student of religious history should realize that each detail mentioned in this passage occurred in precise accordance with the predictions of young Daniel. If this is so, then the final prophetical statement concerning the ten toes of iron and clay must also become a reality. Notice carefully that the iron will still be in existence at the end of time, but in a deteriorated condition. The ten toes have become mixed with clay. Is it not interesting to note that the Roman Empire was never really defeated? It declined through immorality and corruption. Therefore, since the nations of the Roman Empire still exist, it will return to power at the end time in the form of a union of ten Western nations, each of which was a part of the original Roman Empire. The Bible also teaches, "And in the days of these kings [the alignment of the ten Western nations] shall the God of heaven set up a kingdom, which shall never be destroyed" (Daniel 2:44). What does this mean? Simply that Christ is coming soon as King of kings and Lord of lords.

Here's the truth of this scenario: A world church is closely associated with this world government. Revelation 17 portrays a woman sitting upon the beast who rules internationally. John says, "So he carried me away in the spirit into the wilderness: and I saw a woman sit upon a scarlet coloured beast, full of names of blasphemy, having seven heads and ten horns. . . . And upon her forehead was a name written, MYSTERY, BABYLON THE GREAT" (Revelation 17:3, 5). Who is she? Verse 9 provides the answer: "And here is the mind which hath wisdom. The seven heads are seven mountains, on which the woman sitteth." Rome, the eternal city, is situated, geographically, upon seven hills. Thus, it is likely that the Roman Empire in its gloriously revived state will bring the united world church, with headquarters in Rome, into prominence. This church will then reign over the kings of the earth (Revelation 17:18). Pope John Paul II fears that an anti-Pope, totally liberal, could arise at the time of the end. This is Catholic theology and has been believed and propagated by all of the bishops for centuries, including Bishop Sheen and the Jesuit scholar Malachi Martin. It will not be church and state, but church and world unification that will plague our planet at that time.

As we witness the present ecumenical movement on an international scale, the assembling of the ten toes or ten horns in the form of the European Common Market, the search for a leader to control the lawless dissidents of the world, and the promotion of a world number for all humans, we realize that the moment is ripe for the culmination of Bible prophecy. The day of Christ's return is at hand.

I saw the souls of them that were beheaded for the witness of Jesus, and for the word of God, and which had not worshipped the beast, neither his image, neither had received his mark upon their foreheads, or in their hands; and they lived and reigned with Christ a thousand years.

Revelation 20:4

Question 33

What is the nature of the "coming world church"? How will this international institution cooperate with the world identification number "666" and the "image of the beast"?

Revelation 13:11 introduces us to a beast who will serve as ally to the infamous Antichrist. This beast is known as the false prophet or leader of the world church of Revelation 17. Closely identified with the religion of the Roman Empire, this beast will influence the nations of the world to worship the Antichrist—to the extent of setting up an image in the Jewish Temple in Jerusalem. The Lord Jesus referred to this image as the "abomination of desolation" (Matthew 24:15). When this unholy act takes place in the Temple, the true Jewish heart will be broken, because any hint at idolatry flies in the face of the Ten Commandments found in Exodus 20. The second commandment states, "Thou shalt not make unto thee any graven image, or any likeness of any thing that is in heaven above, or that is in the earth beneath, or that is in the water under the earth" (v. 4). The false prophet's religion, however, will have no qualms or conscience with respect to these idols and statues. Thus, the beast will erect an idol in honor of the Antichrist, and the world will be forced to bow to it. Anyone who remains true to the Lord Jesus

Christ, His blood, and the inspiration of the Scriptures will be killed: "I saw the souls of them that were beheaded for the witness of Jesus, and for the word of God, and which had not worshipped the beast, neither his image, neither had received his mark upon their foreheads, or in their hands; and they lived and reigned with Christ a thousand years" (Revelation 20:4).

The Coming World Number

The false prophet of the coming world church will also issue an international identification number. This is a prophecy that is fast becoming reality: "And he had power to give life unto the image of the beast, that the image of the beast should both speak, and cause that as many as would not worship the image of the beast should be killed. And he causeth all, both small and great, rich and poor, free and bond, to receive a mark in their right hand, or in their foreheads: And that no man might buy or sell, save he that had the mark, or the name of the beast, or the number of his name. Here is wisdom. Let him that hath understanding count the number of the beast: for it is the number of a man; and his number is Six hundred threescore and six [or 666]" (Revelation 13:15-18).

What about the Antichrist? Where is he during this time? What connection will he have to the dreaded number 666? I have no doubt that he is alive and presently on the scene, impatiently awaiting his moment to ascend the world throne. When he arises he will set up a world computer system that will keep track of every person on earth, giving each the number 666, according to Revelation 13:6-18. What is the relationship between this number and the

Antichrist? Revelation 13:17 states that 666 is the number of his name. Verse 18 adds, "Here is wisdom. Let him that hath understanding count the number of the beast: for it is the number of a man."

666 and Gematria

Let us look more closely at this number—particularly at some of the scholarly research done on its future impact on humankind. The Rev. J. R. Church, founder and director of the "Prophecy in the News Ministry" in Oklahoma City, Oklahoma, has spent many hours studying the development of the number 666 as it relates to modern society. He says that the word *count* in Revelation 13:18 comes from the Greek word meaning "to compute." Thus, the verse literally states, "Let him that hath understanding compute the number of the beast." To compute a number from a name, one must devise a system of ascribing numeric values to the letters of the alphabet. This procedure is known as gematria.

In attempting to find a gematria for the English alphabet, Church discovered that the ancient Sumerian civilization of modern-day southern Iraq used a sexagesimal system of numerics. The Sumerians lived in the days of Noah and, therefore, constitute the earliest civilization known to archaeologists. Their numbering system was based on a root of six as opposed to our ten. Thus, the common fractions 1/2, 1/3, 1/4, and 1/5 would be written 30/60, 20/60, 15/60, and 12/60. In fact, the *Zondervan Pictorial Encyclopedia of the Bible,* volume 4, implies the likelihood that the number 6 was the base of civilization's first system of computation. Church also discovered that the English alphabet is essentially the same as that of every other language of the world since all tongues found their origin in a common source prior to the tower of Babel. Thus we have *a, b, c* in English; *alpha, beta,* and *gamma* in the Greek; and *aleph, beth,* and *gimel* in the Hebrew.

Reasoning that the Antichrist may have an English name. Church used a gematria formed by adding the number 6 to each letter of the alphabet. Thus, A=6, B=12, C=18, D=24, E=30, F=36, etc. He then proceeded to compute the numerical values of various words associated with Scripture. Identical values were found for the following: Lucifer (444) + hell (222)=666; Lucifer + hades=666; devil + sheol=666; devil + dragon=666; mark + of + beast=666; people + sin=666. Since the image of the beast (Revelation 13:14-15) is undoubtedly a sophisticated computer, Church decided to find the numerical value of the word *computer* (C=18, 0=90, M=78, P=96, U=126, T=120, E=30, R=108). The total: 666! I first noted that his findings were given credence by a statement in the November 1981 issue of *Science Digest.* Harvard theologian Harvey Cox wrote, "The true successors of the [ancient] sorcerers and the alchemists are not the priests and theologians but the physicists and the computer engineers." Certainly this will be true in the case of the Antichrist.

Next, Church began searching for a city whose numerical value would indicate it as a possible location from which the Antichrist will arise. Since Rome plays a central role in Bible prophecy, he began there. However, Rome's gematria totaled only 306. Likewise, the ancient city of Babylon (currently being rebuilt) equals 426 and Jerusalem comes to just 624. Continuing on through the other major cities of the world—London, Paris, Brussels, Moscow, Beijing, Tokyo, and even Washington, D.C.—each effort proved fruitless— until he came to New York City (N=84, E=30, W=138, Y=150, O=90, R=108, K=66, Total: 666).

Although one cannot conclusively prove that New York is the city that will produce the Antichrist, it is chilling to note that it serves as the home of the current world parliament (the United Nations) and is also a base for the international banking industry. Incidentally, just outside New York City is a suburb by the name of Babylon. To cement the validity of Church's research, there was a telephone call from a computer programmer who had been studying the numbering systems of the great empires of world history—Rome, Greece, and Babylon (along with the Medo-Persian Empire, which had the same numbering system as Babylon). The programmer had found that a modern-day name could be formed from the letter values of the number 6 as taken from these three ancient numbering systems. Note this discovery: The number 6 in Roman numerals is made up of the letters VI. The ancient Greek number 6 was taken from the sixth letter of the alphabet, the letter *sigma,* which looks like the English letter *s.* Returning to the Babylonian Empire and its sexagesimal system of numbers, the programmer considered the possibility that its letter A equaled 6. Thus, from the three great world empires of history, he found that the composition of the number 666 spells the word VISA—the precise name of today's most accepted and popular credit card!

What relationship Church's unusual finding might have to the fulfillment of Bible prophecy remains to be seen. I do not set dates, nor do I make predictions. Personally, I am convinced that Christians will not know who the Antichrist is (or from which city he will come) because we will be gone (via the Rapture) before his identity is revealed. Still, it is both interesting and exciting to see the number 666 exposed in so many ways through this system of gematria.

The Image of the Beast

Let's now look at the Antichrist's actual image—certainly to be intricately tied to the computer of all computers—the ultimate masterpiece of the knowledge explosion. Imagine with me the scenario. It is so awe-inspiring that it staggers the imagination. This computer's ability to know virtually everything about everyone is astonishing. We are already sliding down this slippery slope, are we not? Every time you use your special "supermarket" card to receive your discounts, a computer logs an incredible amount of information about you. It knows if you like the color red better than blue; it knows what time of day or night you shop; it knows the products, the brands, the size, and the content of virtually everything you buy—not only during one day's shopping, but also cumulatively. *It is creating a complete dossier on you and your family.* Then, it will, in all probability, sell that privileged information to others who desire to market their products to you. Then when you start receiving direct mail and full-color catalogs touting their products, you, quite unknowingly, may say, "My goodness, this is just what I've been looking for. How clever that someone knew I would like to buy this." Clever indeed. This is "beastly" stuff. And, my friend, it will only become more personally intrusive as we move closer to that glorious day when Christ returns for His own.

Let's look at Revelation 13:15: "And he had power to give life unto the image of the beast, that the image of the beast should both speak, and cause that as many as would not worship the image of the beast should be killed." I hope you are not laughing, scoffing, or mocking what is about to happen. Speaking computers already exist. Years ago, a popular television talk show hosted a talking computer called "Leachum." Millions of Americans saw this robot seated on a desk. It had eyes, arms, legs—and a voice that spoke as clearly as I am able to speak to you! It also had unbelievable knowledge, for it answered any question asked of it. It is called AI—artificial intelligence—and it will soon become the norm.

It will also suggest we are ever closer to the time when Jesus will take us home. We already have microchip architects who are racing to increasingly squeeze information onto wafer-thin silicon. A few pioneering biochemists are plotting a computer revolution that could make obsolete the most advanced circuits dreamed up in the back rooms at Intel and Motorola. Almost unnoticed, the ultimate biological computer has reached the drawing boards. The aim of these systems engineers is to build a computer that can design and assemble itself by using the same mechanism common to all living things. This mechanism is the coding of genetic information in the self-replicating DNA double helix and the translation of this chemical code into the structure of protein.

This biocomputer, implanted in the brain, will sprout nerve projections from its tiny protein facets. The host's neurons would link up with these spindly outgrowths, sending out electrochemical pulses in the brain's own language. The implant would then ideally combine the brain's ability to relate incoming data—to reason—with electronic speed and efficiency. Dr. James McAlear, a specialist in this technology, once said, "We are looking at conductive velocities about a million times faster than nerve cells, circuit switches one hundred million times faster than neuronal junctions, or synapses, and packing densities of the functional circuit elements a million times greater than are formed in the brain. This factor of ten to the twentieth power is truly incomprehensible in terms of any present concept of intelligence. It would be expected that the 'being' of an individual so equipped would live in the computer part, not in the central nervous system. It is also possible that when the corpus perishes, its implant would survive and could be transmitted to a fresh host."[1] What do you think of that? So far, it is a comfortable fit with the specifications for an immortal soul. If you have something that has intelligence and the ability to communicate at high speed, it might well become a single consciousness—a superior, an omnipotent being.

Everything about our society is about to change. *U.S. News & World Report* recently predicted the end of cash. A similar report appeared on the Dow Jones News Service. A European newspaper says the euro dollar will be its replacement. This monetary system, beginning January 1, 1998 will be totally functional by 2002. Note this prediction that eventually everyone will wear a euro transmitter with voice-recognition functions on his or her wrist. This device will permit buyers and sellers to make transactions by keeping tabs of credits and debits—*all without any actual money being exchanged!* In Revelation 13:16-17, we learn that there will come a time, presumably in the near future, when no one in the world will be permitted to buy or sell without receiving a mark on his or her right hand or forehead. In any past generation, such a prophecy would have been unthinkable and impossible to fulfill, even foolish. Today, we have the technology to take us there. *Time* recently ran an article entitled "The Big Bank Theory." In it they stated: "Soon one will be able to store money by a lap computer, VISA card or by a microchip embedded under the skin."[2] We have not yet fully arrived, but when one considers that these predictions were made about the world two thousand years ago—when men lived in houses of stone—there is considerable cause for excitement. Consider the astounding "coincidence" that this technology arrives on the scene in the same generation that witnessed the return of Israel to her land. My friend, it is more than a coincidence: The time of Christ's return is near. Would you not agree that the days of laughing at God's Word are about over? When the apostle John received his word from God nineteen hundred years ago that the end times would produce an image that spoke, I would imagine that even he had difficulty comprehending the message. Now, you and I have witnessed its beginning—and the final countdown to Christ's coming again. Bill Gates just declared: "Within the next decade [ten years] computers will understand and speak human language." It's wake-up time, folks.

For, lo, I will raise and cause to come up
against Babylon an assembly of great nations
from the north country: and they shall set themselves
in array against her.

Jeremiah 50:9

Question 34

The U.S. and Russia: How does their connection play into Rapture events? Why is it said that the U.S. – Russia relationship is "prophecy in fast-forward"?

Not since Jesus ascended into heaven nearly two thousand years ago have the prophecies of the Bible been fulfilled before our eyes on such a grand scale as we observe them today. We see the perilous condition of the human race as described by Paul in 2 Timothy 3:1-5, "This know also, that in the last days perilous times shall come. For men shall be lovers of their own selves, covetous, boasters, proud, blasphemers, disobedient to parents, unthankful, unholy, Without natural affection, trucebreakers, false accusers, incontinent, fierce, despisers of those that are good. Traitors, heady, highminded, lovers of pleasures more than lovers of God; Having a form of godliness, but denying the power thereof: from such turn away."

We see the rise of false prophets and deceiving spirits described in Matthew 24:11. We watch in disbelief as the foundation is laid for the kind of global government depicted in Revelation 13:7. We witness the increase in earthquakes, the changing weather patterns, and the devastation of plagues predicted in Luke 21. Famines are wreaking havoc throughout much of the world as prophesied in Matthew 24:7.

In amazement we watch as tiny Israel continues to move center stage in world politics as predicted in Ezekiel 38:16. Islam forms a coalition of angry neighbors opposed to the existence of Israel as pictured in Psalm 83:4. The kings of the East—China and Japan—move toward rapprochement as one would anticipate in light of Revelation 16:12. In addition, Europe moves closer and closer toward unification as shown in Daniel 7:4-8. The signs are everywhere. We are in the last days—*Jesus is coming soon!* Two parallel developments are especially dramatic: the decline of the United States of America as a world leader and the increasing belligerence and adventurism of Russia. These are major signs.

The United States is still the most powerful nation on earth. It has a proud tradition as a bulwark of liberty and freedom. As the child of Belgian immigrants, I still choke up when my eyes scan the Statue of Liberty, when I pledge allegiance to the flag, or when I sing "America the Beautiful." However, we must remember that God blessed America because it was founded as "one nation under God" and upon sound biblical principles. Today, that righteousness has been debased, and our Judeo-Christian values have been replaced by a truculent secular humanism. Never in history has America been in such a state of degradation, hopelessness, and disrepair. Here are some facts to ponder that speak to our cultural decay:

- 10 million inebriates drink themselves into insensibility daily.

- Another 10 million Americans use and abuse drugs.

- Americans spend $10 billion a year polluting their bodies with tobacco products.

- Another $60 billion a year is thrown away on gambling—on state-sanctioned lotteries as well as illegal betting.

- Sexual promiscuity is condoned and encouraged by government and judicial action.

- Pornography is a multibillion-dollar industry, now taking fresh expression on the Internet with its capacity to invade the most innocent of young minds in the privacy of their own homes.

- Each year millions of children are born out of wedlock, many to girls as young as eleven.

- Abortion has taken the lives of 25 million unborn children since 1973.

- Euthanasia is the next big *legal* killing field, as states adopt laws to permit doctors to "put patients to sleep" like animals.

- Murder claims the lives of 50,000 Americans a year.

No nation can long survive under such sinful circumstances. The Bible says, "Righteousness exalteth a nation: but sin is a reproach to any people" (Proverbs 14:34). Likewise, Psalm 9:17 declares, "The wicked shall be turned into hell, and all the nations that forget God." We are forced to make the case, based on scriptural evidence, that the United States is sliding down the slippery slope toward horrendous judgment. It is true that America is not mentioned in the Bible by name. However, it is also true that "all nations" will suffer judgment in the days before the return of our Lord Jesus Christ (Micah 5:15; Ezekiel 39:21). What's more, Ezekiel 38:13 singles out "Tarshish, with all the young lions," a group of nations that pays a heavy price for coming to the defense of Israel when it is invaded by Russia and a coalition of other nations.

The name Tarshish is found twenty times in the Bible and always refers to the land farthest west of Israel. The text refers to the "merchants of Tarshish" and explains that these people trade goods around the world. Specifically, I believe Tarshish refers to Britain, and all of her young lions refers to the English-speaking world, including the United States. Isaiah 18:1-2 issues a warning to a nation: "Woe to the land shadowing with wings, which is beyond the rivers of Ethiopia: That sendeth ambassadors by the sea, even in vessels of bulrushes upon the waters, saying, Go, ye swift messengers, to a nation scattered and peeled, to a people terrible from their beginning hitherto; a nation meted out and trodden down, whose land the rivers have spoiled."

The nation described in this text is in great difficulty with God because the opening word "woe" in the text is judgmental. This nation has the insignia of wings, similar to America's national emblem, the bald eagle. It is a land that is beyond the sea from Israel. This designation of "beyond Ethiopia" eliminates all of the nations of Europe, Asia, and Africa. It is a land scattered and peeled, meaning it is stretched out and having a large landmass. It is measured and staked out with counties, cities, and states. It is a land with polluted rivers. Does that not sound unmistakably like our precious America? In Jeremiah 50-51, the Holy Spirit talks about a nation called Babylon that is destroyed by an assembly of nations from the north. This is not a reference to ancient Babylon, which was attacked by the Medes and Persians. This Babylon, unlike most other nations, has "a mother." America has a mother: Britain. This "Babylon" is the youngest among the great world powers of the day, just as is America. This Babylon is a wealthy nation of mingled people—a "melting pot" for tens of millions, if you will. It is also a nation that dwells upon many waters. John in the Book of Revelation (chapter 18) also alludes to this nation, a rich land, laden with sins, that has glorified herself and lived deliciously.

That, my friends, is a graphic picture of the United States of America. However, the present hedonistic pleasure craze cannot and will not last forever. America's destruction may come as quick as lightning. We could indeed become the battered and beaten Babylon of the following texts: "For, lo, I will raise and cause to come up against Babylon an assembly of great nations from the north country: and they shall set themselves in array against her ..." (Jeremiah 50:9). Russia is to the north of the USA. "Alas, alas that great city Babylon, that mighty city! for in one hour is thy judgment come" (Revelation 18:10). "Alas, alas that great city, that was clothed in fine linen, and purple, and scarlet, and decked with gold, and precious stones, and pearls! For in one hour so great riches is come to nought. And every shipmaster, and all the company in ships, and sailors, and as many as trade by sea, stood afar off, And cried when they saw the smoke of her burning, saying. What city is like unto this great city! And they cast dust on their heads, and cried, weeping and wailing, saying, Alas, alas, that great city, wherein were made rich all that had ships in the sea by reason of her costliness! For in one hour is she made desolate" (Revelation 18:16-19).

The Great Escape

Only now as we enter a new millennium could a nuclear attack, in one hour's time, obliterate everything our ancestors took two centuries to build. If God has America in mind—and it certainly looks as if He has—then what? Are you prepared for the judgment that may soon hit our nation without warning? We have noted in an earlier question that Russia, the biblical Magog, will attack Israel in the last days. The texts I have cited previously also strongly suggest that America may be victimized simultaneously by an all-out nuclear first strike from Russia.

Crazy thinking, you say? I do not think so. You may keep hearing that the Cold War is over and that Russia is disarming. Nonsense. Russia is more dangerous and unstable than ever before. Its breakaway provinces to the south— where many of the former USSR's nuclear arsenals were in waiting—are now still viable and poised to throw nuclear fire on her enemies. The Russians may know the honeymoon is over, but it would appear that many of our U.S. leaders still have their heads in the sand. Still, money continues to flow like a river to Russia from the West. Conversely, while Russia is modernizing its nuclear arsenal, the U.S. is unilaterally disarming at an unprecedented rate. Funds to support our military are at an all-time low.

Russia remains deceptive in its dealing with the rest of the world. I do not believe the pronouncements of their leaders for a moment. Remember, it was the Russian revolutionary V. I. Lenin who said they would always be willing to take one step backward and two steps forward—feigning weakness, but always aggressively pursuing their global objectives.

The prophet Ezekiel portrays Russia as launching a bloody but ill-fated invasion of the Middle East. It will be the beginning of what I call the "Armageddon campaign." It is important to note this: Armageddon is not one battle but a series of conflicts. Interestingly, one of the loosest canons on the Russian ship is a man named Vladimir Zhirinovsky. He is a Jew-hating fascist. He is also author of a book titled *The Last Dash to the South* (1993) in which he dreams of a future Russian invasion of the Middle East oil fields. (I doubt if Zhirinovsky has ever studied prophecy, yet even the title of his book speaks of the end time!) "Let Russia successfully accomplish *its last dash to the South,*" he writes in his book. "I see Russian soldiers gathering for this last campaign. I see Russian commanding officers in the headquarters of Russian divisions and armies, sketching the lines of troop movements ... I see planes at air bases in the southern districts of Russia. I see submarines surfacing off the shores of the Indian Ocean and landing crafts approaching shores where soldiers of the Russian army are already marching. Infantry combat vehicles are advancing and vast numbers of tanks are on the move. Russia is at last accomplishing its final military campaign." However, he is not through with his saber rattling. He continues: "I say it plainly: when I come to power, there will be a dictatorship. I will beat the Americans in space. I will surround the planet with our space stations, so that they'll be scared of our space weapons. I don't care if they call me a fascist or a Nazi. Workers in Leningrad told me, 'Even if you wear five swastikas, we'll vote for you all the same. You promise a clear plan.' There's nothing like fear to make people work better. The stick, not the carrot. I'll do it all without tanks in the streets. Those who have to be arrested will be arrested quietly at night. I may have to shoot 100,000 people, but the other 300 million will live peacefully. I have the right to shoot 100,000." Pretty volatile stuff, and he plays into the chaos that is common throughout his nation. Could a Russian anti-Semitic leader soon come to power? Time will tell.

- The situation in Russia worsens with each passing day: The economy is in shambles; the aftermath of the terrible Chernobyl nuclear disaster continues to radiate the innocent.

- Russia's fragile economy has moved a step closer to possible collapse amid a deepening financial crisis.

- Russia's foreign debt—$145 billion—is not huge as a percentage of its economy, but lenders around the world are clearly unwilling to put more on the line.

- The cults are going on a rampage in Russia—despite the new "law" that is intended to keep "foreign religions" at bay.

- Bread costs 1,500 rubles, about 8 percent of some monthly salaries.

- The average prices for rent, heat, and electricity often increase as much as 250 percent in one month.

- Workers are not being paid in many enterprises.

- The fee for public transportation has increased 2,000 percent in the past several months—and continues to climb.

I do not know who will be the Russian "Gog," leader of Ezekiel 38, who orders such a campaign, but I do know such a leader is waiting in the wings. When he finally appears, may God have mercy on the world. However, regardless of what appears because of future hostilities between the U.S.

and Russia, God is in control, and at the appointed time He will send His Son to gather His church. That day is soon coming. The Rapture is near.

*The day of the Lord will come as a thief in the night;
in the which the heavens shall pass away with a great
noise, and the elements shall melt with fervent heat, the
earth also and the works that are therein
shall be burned up.*

1 Peter 3:10

Question 35

*What about nuclear war? The Bible says the
"elements shall melt with fervent heat."
Would this refer to nuclear devastation?*

T hese are important questions, often misunderstood
by Christians, especially as we see a Cold War
mentality resurface with the recent underground
testing of atomic bombs by India and Pakistan—the two
latest members of the "nuclear club." Let's look at what the
Bible says about this kind of firepower—and when such
annihilation might occur. We read in 2 Peter 3:10 a clear description of the last days: "But the day of the Lord will come
as a thief in the night; in the which the heavens shall pass
away with a great noise, and the elements shall melt with
fervent heat, the earth also and the works that are therein
shall be burned up." God does not need man's modern inventions to produce the mass devastation mentioned in this
text. Atoms have been here since God created heaven and
earth (Genesis 1:1). Only in our day has science learned to
harness what has always existed. God could have brought
the components together at any time to produce the effects
predicted in this prophecy. This text pictures the renovation of the world. Since God's Word promises a final day of
rest, there can be no complete renovation of the earth until

Christ has reigned for one thousand years. Therefore, this text refers to events to be fulfilled after the Millennium—the thousand-year reign of Christ. However, scores of other texts predict nuclear war for the Tribulation Hour.

Here's the startling truth portrayed in this portion of scripture: Humanity today has the potential to carry out that which prophecy has long predicted for the human race. Because science has harnessed this power, and because God's predictions for the Tribulation Hour promise massive fiery devastation, the hour is most certainly at hand. God is able to carry out everything mentioned in Revelation 8:7 and 9:18. He, the omnipotent One, needs no assistance from the world's Atomic Energy Commissions or the Pentagon. These verses indicate that humans will use atoms during the Tribulation period and at the end of the Millennium. Modem science tells us there are three primary effects of an A- or H-bomb blast. First, there is the tremendous mushrooming effect as it ascends into the heavens upon detonation. Second, as the blast begins its descent, it disintegrates, dissolves, and melts even steel. In fact, a five-hundred-foot steel tower melted into nothingness in the desert of New Mexico during past experiments. Finally, the heat made the same desert a blazing inferno.

Now, observe the statement Peter made under the direction of the Holy Spirit nineteen centuries ago. First, the heavens shall pass away with a great noise. Second, the elements shall melt with fervent heat. God said that the elements would melt. Go to any library and make a study of atomic weaponry. The materials will be classified under the letter *E* under the term *elements*—the very word God used. Think of it! Twentieth-century scientists continue to use the same language God employed nineteen hundred years ago. Finally, Peter states, "The earth also and the works that are therein shall be burned up" (2 Peter 3:10). The three major effects of nuclear detonations are identical to Peter's prophecies and the catastrophic bombardments of earth predicted for the coming Tribulation Hour. In numerous other scriptural texts, undoubtedly, World War HI will be one of incineration. Revelation 9:18 states, "By these three was the third part of men killed, by the fire, and by the smoke, and by the brimstone." I have stood in Japan, near Hiroshima, and remembered with sadness the reports of mayhem and destruction that emanated from the two Japanese cities struck by the atomic bomb during World War II. My mind was troubled. Then I thought about the Tribulation Hour. Zechariah 14:12 pictures an atomic devastation beyond comprehension. The prophet said, "Their flesh shall consume away while they stand upon their feet, and their eyes shall consume away in their holes, and their tongue shall consume away in their mouth." This is the precise effect of humankind's newest weapon—the neutron bomb that destroys people but not property! All of this could take place in the near future. Then, after the millennial reign of Christ, the final atomic renovation of 2 Peter 3:10 will occur.

While believers will not endure the horror of the Tribulation, we must *know the times* so as to be faithful witnesses. That is why we must study and take the time to understand the prophecies in this startling chapter. They are vivid reminders that the coming of our Lord Jesus Christ is near. At a time when the world mocks His return, reveling in its atomic weaponry and false sense of security, and during an era when the sixth day is about to expire, Christ could return momentarily. The clock is ticking away its last fateful seconds. Little time remains. If you do not have a relationship with Jesus Christ and have not accepted Him as your Savior and Lord, you, too, will be left behind with those who refuse to believe. All laughter will end when the fire begins to fall (Genesis 19:14, 24, 25; Luke 17:28-30). It will then be eternally too late. "Behold, now is the accepted time; behold, now is the day of salvation" (2 Corinthians 6:2).

In Conclusion ...

I have an important question for you.

In Matthew 24:3, Christ's disciples asked, "What shall be the sign of thy coming, and of the end of the world [literally, age]?" The Savior proceeded to provide a list of cataclysmic world events, which would both usher in His return and culminate in the Day of the Lord. He added in Luke 21:28, "And when these things begin to come to pass [or begin to occur simultaneously], then look up, and lift up your heads; for your redemption draweth nigh." Concerning this great day, the apostle Paul writes in 1 Thessalonians 5:1-3, "But of the times and the seasons, brethren, ye have no need that I write unto you. For yourselves know perfectly that the day of the Lord so cometh as a thief in the night. For when they shall say, Peace and safety; then sudden destruction cometh upon them."

Never in the pages of world history have we witnessed such a proliferation of the signs Jesus predicted would be in place immediately before His return. No longer are the days of simultaneous war, famine, pestilence, earthquakes, and cultic activity limited to the pages of the Bible. All we need to do today is glance at the morning headlines or listen for five minutes to CNN (or watch the tawdry afternoon television "peep shows") to realize that these signs of Christ's return are in evidence *worldwide* and increasing both in frequency and intensity. Is it any wonder that the scientists who control the famed "doomsday clock" are moving its hands ever closer to midnight?

Prophecy: History Written in Advance

The questions I have tried my best to answer in the preceding pages have dealt with the "tip of the iceberg" when it comes to the stream of end-time events that will usher in the Tribulation—a period of unparalleled terror. I remind you, Christians will *not* be a part of this horrendous time (Revelation 3:10). In answer to your many questions, I have endeavored to deal with most of the major New Testament prophecies that relate to the return of our Lord in the light of current international events. *Remember that prophecy is simply history written in advance.* It is God's declaration and description of future events. As such, prophecy cannot, has not, and will never fail in even the smallest detail until all has been fulfilled. The day of that ultimate fulfillment is upon us. My personal prayer is that, upon completing this book, you will renew your vow of love, service, and allegiance to the Savior. If you do not yet know the Lord of lords and King of kings, it is my earnest prayer that you will open your heart and your life to Jesus today. Do not be left behind. Do not say, "I wish I had taken the words of prophecy more seriously."

Will it be easy for us in the years *before* the Tribulation? I think not. We will still be compelled to deal with runaway crime, abortions, drug abuse, plagues, pestilence, AIDS, wars, and rumors of wars, and an unprecedented hostility toward the gospel. The question is, Will you be strong in your love for Christ, or will you sell your birthright for a few thrills during the challenging times that are sure to lie ahead? Will you be an end-time hero for the faith? Alternatively, will you be found wanting? The apostle John, thrown into a cauldron of boiling oil, survived the painful ordeal but was disfigured for life and banned to the isle of Patmos. The beloved apostle Paul was beheaded. Two of the New Testament writers, Jude and Peter, were crucified. Another Gospel writer, James, was battered to death with a fuller's club.

Now let us look at the larger picture: Soon the great hour will have arrived, and all God's children will be present as the investigation begins. What will you say as you stand with such an array of heroes—believers who gave their all and who proved their first love for Christ during an entire lifetime and even unto death? Only you know the answer. Christ's return may be tomorrow, next week, next month, or next year. We do not know the day or the hour when Jesus will break through the blue to call us home. However, we do know that it is near, even at the doors. Therefore, my closing questions to you are: Are you ready for Christ's imminent return? Could you bear the investigative judgment if it were to take place tomorrow? Would you be ashamed, embarrassed, red-faced, even brokenhearted? Would tears of sorrow flow from your eyes for an entire millennial age? Is your present disobedience worth such heartache? Would you not rather serve God with all your heart and hear Him say with a loud voice: "Well done, thou good and faithful servant" (Matthew 25:21)? It is not too late to make a change, to reverse your lifestyle, and put

Christ first in your life. If you do not know the Savior, I urge you to obey John 1:12 and Romans 10:13. If you are away from the Lord, I plead with you to act upon 1 John 1:9, "If we confess our sins, he is faithful and just to forgive us our sins, and to cleanse us from all unrighteousness." Do it. Make the right decision. Then live the remainder of your days for Him, short as those days might be. It will be worth it all when we see Jesus.

Maranatha! The King is coming!

Notes

Read This First

1. Ephraem the Syrian, A.D. 373. On the Last Times, the Antichrist, and the End of the World,

Question Three

1. Gerald B. Stanton, "A Critique of the Pre-Wrath Rapture Theory," *Biblical Perspectives,* 4, no. 1, 2 (January-February 1991).

2. Tim LaHaye, No *Fear of the Storm* (Sisters, Ore.: Muknomah, 1992), 101.

Question Five

1. David Jeremiah, *Escape the Coming Night* (Dallas, Tex.: Word, 1990), 117-18.

Question Seventeen

1. H. L. Willmington, *The King Is Coming* (Wheaton. 111: Tyndale, 1991), 71.

Question Thirty-three

1. Kathleen McAuliffe, "Biochip Revolution," *Omm.*

2. Joshua Cooper Ramo, "The Big Bank Theory," *Time* 151, no. 16 (1998): 1-5.

Lamb and Lion Ministe

PO Box 919.

Mkim TX 75070

Offer 71. $20

972 736 3567

8a sp

CST www.
Lamblion.com